Fruit of the Spiri

Fruit of the Spirit
Stephen F. Winward

Inter-Varsity Press, Leicester, England
William B. Eerdmans Publishing Company,
Grand Rapids, Michigan

Inter-Varsity Press
38 De Montfort Street, Leicester LE1 7GP, England
Wm. B. Eerdmans Publishing Company
255 Jefferson S.E., Grand Rapids, MI 49503

First published in England 1981
Reprinted 1984

British Library Cataloguing in Publication Data

Winward, Stephen Frederick
Fruit of the Spirit.
I. Title
248.2'9   BT123

ISBN 0 85110 430 4

Library of Congress Cataloging in Publication Data

Winward, Stephen F.
Fruit of the spirit.

1. Virtues.   2. Gifts, Spiritual.   I. Title.
BV4630.W56   1984   241'.4   83-25328

ISBN 0-8028-0003-3

Set in 10/11 Baskerville
Phototypeset by Nuprint Services Ltd, Harpenden, Herts
Printed by William Collins Sons and Co Ltd, Glasgow

Inter-Varsity Press is the publishing division of the Universities and Colleges Christian Fellowship (formerly the Inter-Varsity Fellowship), a student movement linking Christian Unions in universities and colleges throughout the United Kingdom and the Republic of Ireland, and a member movement of the International Fellowship of Evangelical Students. For information about local and national activities write to UCCF, 38 De Montfort Street, Leicester LE1 7GP.

Contents

Abbreviations

Bible references which are not taken from the Revised
Standard Version are quoted with the following
abbreviations:

AV	*Authorized Version (King James')*, 1611
GNB	*Good News Bible*, 1976
JB	*Jerusalem Bible*, 1966
J.B. Phillips	*The New Testament in Modern English*, 1958
Moffatt	*A New Translation of the Bible*, 1935
NEB	*New English Bible*, 1972

Preface

This book is about Christian character, a subject of supreme importance. For making people, and making them like Christ, is the climax and goal of God's creative activity. That was the end he planned in the beginning. According to God's eternal purpose, writes Paul, Christians have been chosen, called and set apart to become like his Son. Through his Spirit, God is ceaselessly at work in the world, shaping people into the likeness of Jesus Christ. We can define the people of God in terms of that purpose of God. Christians are the people who, having accepted Christ, seek to live in accordance with his character and are being transformed by the Holy Spirit into his likeness. We are here on earth to become like Christ, in heaven we shall be like Christ.

This twentieth century has witnessed the rise and expansion of the pentecostal and charismatic movements. As a result, great emphasis has been laid on the recovery and use of the gifts of the Spirit. In his day, the apostle Paul welcomed and valued all these charismatic gifts. But he shifted the emphasis. There are lower and higher gifts. Better than the spectacular gifts are those which are of greater use in building up the community. And better even than the exercise of the higher gifts is the more excellent way of love. Love is *the* fruit of the Spirit, and all the other eight fruits of the Spirit are aspects of love. So Paul shifts the emphasis from the gifts to the fruit of the Spirit. The gifts are the abilities the Spirit entrusts to Christians for the common good; the fruits are the virtues and graces the Spirit produces in the character of

Christians. It is no part of Paul's purpose to enhance the fruits by devaluing the gifts. Both matter; it is not a case of either-or, but of both-and. In our churches today we need both the fruits and the gifts. It is, however, the fruit of the Spirit which is of supreme importance. Apart from Christ-like character, gifts are useless; they can be harmful and destructive. We need to recover this apostolic valuation and emphasis. There has been a spate of books on the *charismata*, the gifts of the Spirit. It is high time to emphasize the paramount importance of the fruits of the Spirit.

Since the fruits of the Spirit are the virtues of Christ, this book is about the character of Christ. We shall outline his character as portrayed in the letters and the gospels of the New Testament. Afterwards, as we look at each of the nine fruits of the Spirit, we must keep our eyes on him, the source of all these graces. For it is the character of Christ which the Holy Spirit produces in Christians.

It will also be necessary to study other parts of the Bible in order to discover the original meaning of the nine Greek words, translated into English as love, joy, peace, patience, kindness, goodness, faithfulness, gentleness, self-control. For words, like the currency, are often devalued with the passage of time. Not only can the meaning of a word be seriously weakened, it can also be subtly changed. An ancient oil-painting may need to be cleaned and restored, if its original colour and beauty are to be seen. We can restore the nine words by studying the way in which they are used in various and significant contexts in the Old and New Testaments. The dictionary can tell us what the words mean today; the Bible alone can tell us what they meant to Paul. So this book has a lot of the Bible in it.

To stay in the Bible, however, is not sufficient, for we are called to follow in the footsteps of Christ in the contemporary world. So we shall let the word *today* keep on sounding in our ears. After having studied in the Bible the meaning of the words for the nine fruits of the Spirit, we shall in each case move on and out into the life of our world. For it is today, here and now, at home and at work, in the world and in the church, that we are called to follow Christ. The Spirit will produce in us the virtues of Christ in our present circumstances, within our existing relationships, as we face today's tasks and problems. We shall endeavour to show what it means to be a Christian, loving and joyful, peaceable and patient, kind and good, faithful, gentle and controlled, in these closing decades of the twentieth century.

Also to be kept in mind, together with the word *today*, is that little word *how*! For it is not sufficient to describe the Christian character, or to provide attractive examples of it. Most of all, we need to know *how* to live the Christian life. The Christian character is entirely the creation of the Holy Spirit, who produces in us the fruits of the Spirit which are the virtues of Christ. But the Spirit doesn't do this work apart from us; he takes us into partnership. If so, then *how* do we co-operate with the Spirit? That is the crucial question to be answered.

1 The fruit of the Spirit

What do you want?

You are, I hope, starting to read this book because you want to see the fruit of the Spirit – love, joy, peace, patience, kindness, goodness, faithfulness, gentleness, self-control – in your life. Good! But how much do you want it? Take a piece of paper and a pencil. At the top of the paper write out the question once put by the Lord Jesus to a person in need. 'What do you want me to do for you?' (Mk. 10:51). Then, set down three things you want more than anything else in the world. Provided you are not suffering from what R. L. Stevenson called 'the malady of not wanting', you may be able to identify your primary desires and long-term objectives. Now look at your three chief desires. Do you want to have, to do or to be? Do they refer to possessions, achievements or character? When the question 'What would you like me to give you?' was put to young Solomon, he asked for a quality of character. 'Give me the wisdom I need' (1 Ki. 3:5,9 GNB). I hope that one at least of your three desires has to do with character. For the grand purpose of God is that we should 'become like his Son' (Rom. 8:29 GNB). No Christian could possibly have a greater ambition. So, happy is the person who can truthfully give this answer to the question put by Jesus, 'What I want you to do for me, Lord, is to make me a loving, joyful, peaceable, patient, kind, good, faithful, gentle, disciplined Christian.'

What a forlorn hope! To be like Christ is not the chief aim of many Christians. Not because they are unattracted by the ideal, but because they are discouraged by their own faults and failures. If we use the nine fruits of the Spirit as a standard for self-examination, we may perhaps see in our lives some of the exact opposites. Love, joy, peace? but we are cold and unconcerned, moody and gloomy, worried and quarrelsome. Patience, kindness, goodness? but we are often bad-tempered and irritable, unfriendly and unhelpful, mean and evil. Faithfulness, gentleness, self-control? but sometimes we are unreliable and disloyal, ill-mannered and harsh, slack and undisciplined. To see ourselves as we are takes the heart out of us, saps our vitality. We can become so discouraged that we lose all incentive to change. 'Count me out,' you may say. 'Becoming like Christ may well have been the aim of those saints with a halo, but it's obviously not for me.'

There is, in fact, no need for any Christian to be discouraged or to despair of ever becoming like Christ. For God, the Father, the Son and the Holy Spirit, has worked, is working and will work to that end. It is the eternal purpose of God the Father; he has chosen and called us in order that we might 'be conformed to the image of his Son' (Rom. 8:29). As a carpenter, Jesus must often have dealt skilfully with wood, rough and gnarled. We may be unpromising material, but his skilful hands can make something of us. In the words of an old prayer, we can keep on asking him to do just that. 'Jesus, Master, Carpenter of Nazareth, who at the last upon the cross, through wood and nails, did purchase man's whole salvation; wield well your tools in this your workshop, that we who come to you rough hewn may be fashioned to a truer beauty by your hand.' Reverting from carpentry to horticulture (for fruit grows on trees and plants) we can be sure, like Paul, that God will bring to completion the good work he has begun in us. We shall eventually 'be filled with the fruits of righteousness', *i.e.* 'with the truly good qualities which only Jesus Christ can produce' (Phil. 1:6, 11 RSV and GNB). It's encouraging to know that *we* don't have to produce them. *Jesus* produces them by the activity of the Holy Spirit within us. True, it takes a long time. That's because it is fruit. You don't expect to get apples a month or two after planting an apple tree. And so, what God wills and for which he works

14

can be ours if we really want it. That's why we must start with the question... 'What do you want?'

When he was old, the poet Samuel Coleridge wrote a letter to his young godson. He wanted to tell him, in order of importance, about the four greatest blessings he had found in his life. He singles out for special mention good health, honest work which provides enough income to live on, and kind, faithful and loving friends (were any of these among your three chief wants?). 'But the greatest of all blessings is to *be* indeed a Christian.'[1] Having is important, doing is even more important but *being* matters most of all. 'What do you want?' Can you answer the question in the words of a negro spiritual? 'Lord, I want to be a Christian in my heart... Lord, I want to be like Jesus in my heart.' It's a matter of motivation.

Trees and fruit

Speaking of motivation, how fortunate it is that fruit is usually appetizing and attractive. For it's not only fruit from the forbidden tree that is 'good for food and... a delight to the eyes and... to be desired' (Gn. 3:6). No doubt Paul had this alluring aspect of the word *fruit* in mind when he called the various qualities of the character of Christ, the fruits of the Spirit. And so, before we turn to the symbolic use of the word, let us first look at some of the fruits of the earth. For the literal use of a word comes before and underlies the symbolic use. Paul would be familiar with the various kinds of fruit mentioned in the Bible; olives, figs, grapes, pomegranates, dates, citrons, melons, mulberries. For British readers the word *fruit* conjures up pictures of apples and pears, plums and cherries, blackberries and raspberries, black and red currants, gooseberries and strawberries, apricots and peaches. And in our shops and supermarkets we are able to see and buy fruits from all over the world: oranges and bananas, for example, are as familiar to us as apples and pears. So the word *fruit*, used literally, brings to mind a wealth of images. It has pleasant associations; it appeals to the senses, of sight, touch, smell and especially of taste. It belongs to the garden, the orchard, the fields; to the world of

15

beauty, colour and fragrance, of fertility, growth and maturity. And growth suggests slowness. Following bud, leaf and flower, fruits ripen slowly. But when they are ripe, they satisfy the hunger and sometimes the thirst of man and beast.

All these rich, varied and pleasant associations of the word *fruit*, used literally, are carried over into its symbolical use in the Bible. For not only the products of plants and trees, fruit, but also the products of human nature, can be beautiful and useful, pleasant and satisfying. Not that all the products of human nature are good. The quality of the fruit depends on the nature of the tree. 'Are grapes gathered from thorns, or figs from thistles? So, every sound tree bears good fruit, but the bad tree bears evil fruit' (Mt. 7:16-17). Like a tree, a person bears fruit. Bad people, bad fruit: good people, good fruit. The fruit which a person bears, whether good or bad, is of three main kinds. Jesus said that the *words* of a man are the fruit (*i.e.* the product, the outcome) of what that person is. As 'the tree is known by its fruit', so is the man or woman known by his or her words. 'For out of the abundance of the heart the mouth speaks. The good man out of his good treasure brings forth good, and the evil man out of his evil treasure brings forth evil' (Mt. 12:33-35). Jesus also taught that *deeds* are fruit. 'You will know them by their fruits' was spoken of false prophets who did 'many mighty works' (Mt. 7:15-23). What they didn't do was God's will. When John the Baptist said to the people, 'If you are repentant, produce the appropriate fruits', he went on to tell them of six good things they should do (Lk. 3:8-14 JB). But fruit is more than words or deeds; it includes the *qualities of character* from which those words and deeds issue, 'for the fruit of light is found in all that is good and right and true' (Eph. 5:9). Outstanding among the 'truly good qualities' of Christian character are the nine fruits of the Spirit. They include all three, words, deeds and virtues. For love, joy, peace and all the fruits of the Spirit are revealed in what we say, in what we do and in what we are.

Jotham, son of Gideon, once told a story about trees and fruit. The trees of the forest came together to choose a king for themselves. The invitation 'You come and be our king' was extended, in succession, to the olive-tree, the fig-tree and the grape-vine. All three trees refused on the same ground. They couldn't do two things at once, so they preferred to do the more important of the two. The function of a tree is not to rule but to bear fruit. Usefulness comes before kingship; bearing fruit is more important than exercising authority (Jdg. 9:8-13). Bearing the fruit of good words, good deeds and the virtues and graces of a Christ-like character should be given absolute priority in our lives.

Life in Christ

How is this fruit produced? We have already seen that the perfect example of Christ can be deeply discouraging to us. When we examine ourselves by the standard of his mature manhood we lose heart. On the other hand fruits are attractive and alluring. When we look away from ourselves to the qualities of the character of Christ, we are attracted and long to become like him. But, despite the attraction, the hope of becoming like Christ would still be a forlorn hope if he were only an example before us or a companion alongside us. The good news is that he offers to come and live *in* us and change us from the inside. It's when we are in Christ and he is in us that the fruits, the good qualities of character and all the words and deeds which issue from them, are produced.

Now a person comes to be in Christ by hearing and believing the gospel. When the Son of God, Christ crucified and risen, is portrayed before our eyes, and we respond with faith, then Christ comes to live in us and we live in him. This trusting and entrusting our lives to the Saviour and Lord is the beginning of the process of producing fruit. Having come into Christ by faith we must then continue to live in him. For a Christian is 'a man in Christ' (2 Cor. 12:2). That phrase 'in Christ' (or its equivalents, *e.g.* 'in him') is used 164 times in Paul's letters. It describes our continuing relationship with the risen and glorified Lord who was crucified. A bird flies in the air, a fish swims in the sea, a plant grows in the soil, a Christian lives in Christ. The prophet Jeremiah describes a stately tree growing near a stream. Because it sends out roots to the water its leaves stay green and it keeps on bearing fruit

(Je. 17:8). Rooted in the soil, a tree takes in water containing salts and chemicals and this nourishment circulates through the sapwood into the trunk, branches and leaves. The sequence is water, roots, leaves, fruit. Rooted in and taking in from the soil, the tree bears fruit. By faith we are rooted and grounded in Christ, and as by faith we keep on taking in from him life and nourishment, we keep on bearing fruit.

This life in Christ is described in the allegory of the vine and the branches, in which Jesus teaches us four things about fruit-bearing (Jn. 15:1-17). Here the verb *menō*, to abide, to remain, to dwell, is used ten times. Abiding is the recurring theme. As branches bear fruit because they abide in the vine, so Christians bear fruit because they abide in Christ. 'He who abides in me, and I in him, he it is that bears much fruit.' This union with Christ through faith is continued and maintained through obedience. 'If you keep my commandments, you will abide in my love, just as I have kept my Father's commandments and abide in his love.' This obedience is inseparable from mutual love. 'This is my commandment, that you love one another as I have loved you.' We cannot be Christians, people living 'in Christ', unless we are also brothers and sisters, people living 'in love'. To abide in Jesus we must also cherish and keep his words. 'If you abide in me, and my words abide in you'...the two go together. If we order our lives in accordance with his words, his teaching and commandments, and with the Word, the total self-disclosure of God in Christ, then we shall bear much fruit.

In this allegory the Lord Jesus also describes the fruit, the results of dwelling in him. Our prayers are effectual. That is because they are offered 'in the name', *i.e.* in harmony with the revealed nature, the character of God in Christ. 'If you abide in me, and my words abide in you, ask whatever you will, and it shall be done for you.' The range of a Christian's influence is extended through intercession, and bears much fruit in the lives of others. Bearing fruit is also making disciples. The disciples of Jesus are sent out on a mission; the result will be a harvest of people. 'I chose you and appointed you that you should go and bear fruit and that your fruit should abide.' Those who are in Christ influence others; by

18

their words of witness, their deeds of lovingkindness and qualities of Christian character, they are used to win men for Christ. Winning people is bearing fruit. Through these same words, deeds and virtues, as through their effective prayers and faithful witness, through the total fruitfulness of committed Christians, God is advertised, exhibited, made known. 'By this my Father is glorified, that you bear much fruit, and so prove to be my disciples.'

In his book *The Wind in the Willows*, Kenneth Grahame describes the meeting between Mole and Rat, whose little home is on the banks of a river. Mole, who has never seen a river before, is lost in wonder. He says to Rat, 'You must think me very rude; but all this is so new to me. So – this – is – a – River!' '*The* River', corrected the Rat. 'And you really live by the river? What a jolly life!' 'By it and with it and on it and *in* it', said the Rat. 'It's my world, and I don't want any other.' Living *with* Christ, depending *on* Christ is not sufficient. If we are to enjoy life to the full, and if we are to bear much fruit, then we must live *in* Christ. That is the open secret of fruit-bearing.

The work of the Spirit

It is by the Holy Spirit that Christ lives in our hearts, and it is by the activity of the Holy Spirit that he produces the fruit. That is apparent if we emphasize the last three words in the phrase 'the fruit *of the Spirit*'. The work the Spirit does within us is indicated by the adjective *Holy* which qualifies the noun *Spirit*. After making us alive to God through Jesus Christ (regeneration), the Spirit works to make us holy, to change us into the likeness of Jesus Christ (sanctification). That is God's eternal plan. 'For God knew his own before ever they were, and also ordained that they should be shaped to the likeness of his Son, that he might be the eldest among a large family of brothers' (Rom. 8:29 NEB). It's because the work of the Spirit is to make us like Christ that we must look carefully at what Christ was like. That is why the next chapter is on the character of Christ.

This work of the Spirit, making us holy, is both a completed act and a continuing process. How can it be both? On leaving school at sixteen, John Smith received a prize, a beautifully bound copy of *The Complete Works of William Shakespeare*. It was all his, the comedies, histories, tragedies, all twenty-seven plays. But although he owned it he didn't possess it. The volume stayed on the shelf unopened, unread, unappreciated. John was over twenty when, on impulse, he took down the book and began to read *The Tempest*. He was surprised by joy. During the next four years he read one play after another with steadily increasing pleasure and appreciation. He was now possessing what had belonged to him for years; he was progressively making his own a treasure which had already been given to him.

Holiness is both a gift and a task. It is given at the outset; to become a Christian is to be sanctified. 'You were washed, you were sanctified, you were justified in the name of the Lord Jesus Christ and in the Spirit of our God' (1 Cor. 6:11). When the Corinthians heard and believed the gospel they had themselves washed (baptized), they were dedicated, made to belong to God (sanctified), and they were put right with and accepted by God (justified). These were not three successive acts but three aspects of one and the same act. They were cleansed, consecrated and accepted in the name of the Lord Jesus Christ by the operation and power of the Spirit of God. So it is with us. At conversion and baptism we are sanctified, separated to and possessed by God. What a great encouragement to have it all as a gift to start with! Having received the gift, the new nature, we then set out on the long journey towards the ultimate goal, complete Christlikeness. This task of 'possessing our possessions' is described in the paradox 'be what you are'. Having 'put on the Lord Jesus Christ', we accept the obligation and task of becoming like him. We are to 'strive…for the holiness without which no one will see the Lord' (Heb. 12:14).

'Try to live a holy life'

'Strive for the holiness' – but surely there is no need to strive! Since changing us into the likeness of Christ is entirely a work of the Holy Spirit then surely there is nothing we have to do. As an old hymn has it, 'it is not try, but trust'. That contrast, however, is not found in the New Testament. There, the Christian life is described not only by verbs denoting receptivity: hearing, trusting, receiving, resting, relying, but also by verbs denoting activity: striving, working, running, fighting, casting away, putting on, *etc.* The work of the Spirit within us depends for its continuance and completion upon our obedient response, our co-operation. 'Work out your own salvation with fear and trembling; for God is at work in you, both to will and to work for his good pleasure' (Phil. 2:12-13). God at work in us is the Holy Spirit. Human effort by itself is futile; inspired and enabled by the Spirit, it is fruitful. In a number of places in his letters Paul states both sides of this partnership. 'I am toiling strenuously with all the energy and power of Christ at work in me' (Col. 1:29 NEB). It would be a disastrous misunderstanding of this partnership if we took it to mean that the Lord does some and we do some of the work. The Lord does it all, with us, in us, through us. God's enabling grace and man's strenuous effort belong together. Agriculture supplies a good analogy. Because 'the earth produces of itself', 'the farmer waits for the precious fruit of the earth' (Mk. 4:28; Jas. 5:7). He certainly doesn't try to produce it! Yet before the waiting and the growth comes the ploughing, harrowing, sowing; and after comes the harvesting, threshing, grinding, baking. We work for our daily bread which is a gift of God the Creator. As with God's gifts in creation, so with his gifts in Christ. Man must work to appropriate that which God alone can give. So 'try to live a holy life, because no one will see the Lord without it' (Heb. 12:14 GNB).

Four ways of working with the Spirit

1. *Attention* There are four ways of working with the Spirit which are of outstanding importance. First, we must establish the habit of attending to the things of God. 'Those who live as the Spirit tells them to, have their minds controlled by what the Spirit wants' (Rom. 8:5 GNB). The true function of the

human will, inspired and enabled by the Spirit, is to direct the attention to God in Christ. We can't make ourselves like Christ but we can keep on directing our attention to him. And that is what matters, for we become like that to which we constantly attend. What is decisive is the attitude of the mind. 'Set your minds.' That's the appeal of the apostle to those already risen with Christ. Our minds and hearts must be set on the risen, ascended and reigning Lord (Col. 3:1-2). We must run the race of life with resolution, eyes fixed upon Jesus (Heb. 12:2). When exposed to light from a sunlit object, the chemical compound on the film of a camera is changed. The Christian should keep on exposing himself to the light of the knowledge of God's glory in the face of Christ. We do the exposing: the Spirit will do the changing. 'We, with our unveiled faces contemplating the brightness, all grow brighter and brighter as we are turned into the image that we reflect; this is the work of the Lord who is Spirit' (2 Cor. 3:18 JB margin). Get your attention off yourself on to the Lord! For as Teresa of Avila put it, 'We shall advance more by contemplating divinity than by keeping our eyes fixed on ourselves.'

2. *Devotion* The main way of directing our attention to the Lord is by the three devotional habits of recollection, private prayer and public worship. Practise the presence of God; turn your thoughts to him again and again during the course of the day. Near to the beginning and the end of each day, set aside quiet times to read and meditate on God's Word and to speak to him in prayer. Join every Sunday with the people of God in praise and prayer, to listen to the word taught and preached and to celebrate the sacrifice and victory of Christ in the sacrament. Christians, like their master, are transfigured at prayer (Lk. 9:29). This is one of the main ways in which we obey Christ's command, 'Abide in me and I in you.' 'All forms of Christian worship, all forms of Christian discipline, have this as their object. Whatever leads to this is good; whatever hinders this is bad; whatever does not bear on this is futile.'[2]

3. *Restraint* No Christian on earth is entirely Christlike; that belongs to the age to come. In this present overlap of the two ages, the old self-centred man and the new Christ-centred man are both alive and active. Between the two there is tension, conflict, warfare. 'You have taken off the old self with its habits and have put on the new self' (Col. 3:9-10 GNB). But because, in fact, that old self is still very much alive, and keeps on asserting himself, we have to keep on putting him to death. Baptized once for all into union with Christ in his death and resurrection, we have to live out our baptism by dying daily to sin and rising daily with Christ to newness of life. The vices of the old life have to be 'put off' and the virtues of the new life 'put on'. Stripping off, putting to death, killing, means that we must check, restrain, refuse, deny the thoughts, desires and impulses which arise from the old self-centred nature. This is painful. To say 'no' frustrates and hurts. But it's essential to that growth in holiness without which no-one can see the Lord.

4. *Practice* As well as the negative discipline of 'putting off' there is the positive one of 'putting on'. We are to put into practice the virtues of the new life. A bad tree cannot bear good fruit and a man who has not been raised with Christ to the new life cannot grow in holiness. Bad men don't become good men by performing virtuous acts. On the other hand, if a man is a new creation, has been born again, then his virtues will develop and grow by practice. In the context of the new life practice makes perfect. For just as exercise is essential to the health and growth of the body, so practice is essential to the growth and health of the personality. Love, for example, grows by means of the acts which express it. So with patience; only when we practise being patient in all those relationships and situations which tempt us to be impatient will we become steadily more patient. Again, the gift of self-control becomes our possession when we exercise it. In fact there is no virtue, received as a gift, which is not increased by practice. In that paradox of the Christian life, 'be what you are', *'be'* is a command. It spells activity, effort, striving. We are urged to 'put on' the garments of Christ, to 'put on' the armour of

God. He supplies the garments and the armour, the virtues and the graces, but he doesn't dress us! It's up to us to put them on. We must now turn to the context in which all this activity is to take place, the fellowship.

Bearing fruit in the community

The Christian character flowers and bears fruit in the Christian community. The virtues are not produced by the Spirit in the isolated individual but in the fellowship which the Spirit creates and indwells. 'No man is an Island, entire of itself.'[3] Nor is a Christian a Robinson Crusoe existing in complete isolation on a desert island. To become a Christian is to enter the fellowship. At baptism, by the action of the Holy Spirit, we are sanctified and brought into the body of Christ. 'For Christ is like a single body with its many limbs and organs, which, many as they are, together make up one body. For indeed we were all brought into one body by baptism, in the one Spirit, whether we are Jews or Greeks, whether slaves or free men, and that one Holy Spirit was poured out for all of us to drink' (1 Cor. 12:12-13 NEB). In joining us to Christ the Holy Spirit joins us at the same time to all our brothers and sisters in Christ. He creates *koinōnia*, sharing, partnership in Christ. To be in Christ is to be in the fellowship, created, maintained and indwelt by the Holy Spirit.

We can illustrate the corporate setting of the virtues of Christian character. In the Old Testament the vine is the symbol of the people of God. 'You brought a grapevine out of Egypt; you drove out other nations and planted it in their land' (Ps. 80: 8 GNB). Often the figure of the vine is used in the Old Testament to represent Israel's failure. When Jesus says, 'I am the true vine', he is deliberately contrasting himself and his disciples with Israel, the unfruitful vine. 'He is the true Israel, the faithful Remnant: He is in his own Person the whole people of God.'[4] Christ in his disciples and the disciples in Christ – that is the vine. Fruit is produced in the community of those who are in Christ.

All the fruits of the Spirit, all nine virtues, are communal, the graces of life in community. A few examples will suffice. *Love* is a word rarely used in the New Testament of our love for God; it's commonly used of our love for one another, made possible by God's love for us. True, we do have *peace* with God through our Lord Jesus Christ but he also makes peace between us. *Fidelity* and *gentleness* are virtues required and shown mainly in our relationships with others. While a Christian must indeed *control* himself, he must do so primarily in relationship to others and for their sakes. In short, all nine virtues have reference to our personal relationships, especially within the Christian fellowship. The tree on which these fruits are produced is the community.

How we relate to and get on with others is the supreme test of Christian character. Progress in holiness can best be measured not by the length of time we spend in prayer, not by the number of times we go to church, not by the amount of money we contribute to God's work, not by the range and depth of our knowledge of the Bible, but rather by the quality of our personal relationships. A husband can come home from church and shout at his wife because the dinner isn't ready. A minister can have profound knowledge of the Bible and be at cross-purposes with his church officers. A man of prayer can be callously indifferent to the needs of others. A Christian who gives generously to God's work can be cantankerous and disruptive in the fellowship. This is the most searching test of Christlikeness. How do I get on with my parents, my children, my husband, my wife, my brothers and sisters, my relatives, the people I work for and with every day, my friends, my neighbours, the people I dislike, the people who rub me up the wrong way? Above all, how do I get on with my brothers and sisters in Christ in the church fellowship? It is as we live in these relationships, and it is for a life to be lived within these relationships, that the Holy Spirit produces and perfects in us the qualities of character for life in community.

Not fruits but fruit

It is significant that the apostle Paul writes of the works

25

(pl.) of the flesh, and of the fruit (sing.) of the Spirit (Gal. 5:19, 22). Evil is plural, goodness singular. The apostle names fifteen 'works of the flesh'. Since the list ends with the words 'and the like', it is intended to be typical, not exhaustive. There are many more. Sin produces an unholy brood. The evil man is like the madman of Gerasa who said, 'My name is Legion; for we are many' (Mk. 5:9). Sin disrupts and disintegrates; the sinner 'goes to pieces'. Like the jumbled-up pieces of a jig-saw puzzle his life is split into fragments. The Spirit fits the pieces together into a meaningful picture. He makes whole. Reconciling us to God and to one another, the Spirit integrates and unifies the personality in Christ. As there is one Spirit, so there is one fruit of our response to the Spirit. The one reality to which we respond is love, 'the love of God in Christ Jesus our Lord…poured into our hearts through the Holy Spirit which has been given to us' (Rom. 8:39; 5: 5). This love of God, of the Father, the Son and the Holy Spirit, is the fruit. So there are not nine separate fruits but one fruit of the Spirit. Each one of the other eight graces or virtues – joy, peace, patience, kindness, goodness, faithfulness, gentleness, self-control – is an aspect of love.

The many are aspects of the one. There is one rainbow and many colours. A white ray of sunlight, falling upon prismatic raindrops, is broken up into all the colours of the spectrum, red, orange, yellow, green, blue, indigo, violet. The one composite ray of light is dispersed and appears (Latin *spectrum* means appearance) to our eyes as many colours. The Holy Spirit, the radiant light of the love of God in Christ, falling upon our lives in their various relationships and situations, is dispersed and appears to our eyes as multi-coloured, made up of many graces and virtues. Because there are nine I shall often be compelled to use the plural and write of the fruits of the Spirit. But in making this concession to grammar we must always keep in mind that behind the appearance of multiplicity there is the single reality, the fruit.

This has important implications for the growth of Christian character. Mr Badman, because his life is split up into fragments, may set his mind on one of 'the works of the flesh' so that it becomes a habit. On the other hand, Mr Goodman cannot acquire the various virtues in isolation. For since the love of God in Christ includes all the virtues, in responding to that love he receives all the virtues. If, let's say, I am deficient in joy then I shall not become joyful by concentrating on becoming joyful. For joy is the fruit of a relationship from which all the other virtues likewise spring. If I lack patience I shall be sadly misguided if I focus my attention on becoming patient: it should be focused on the one source of all the graces, patience included. In the same way, self-control is the fruit of Christ-control. This doesn't mean, as we have already seen, and shall see more fully in later chapters, that there is no place for the practice or exercise of the virtues, if they have already been received as gifts. What it does mean is that there can be no growth in or appropriation of a virtue, a fruit, apart from the growth and development of all the other virtues of the character as a whole. It is in the context of a continuing and ever-deepening response to the love of God in Christ that all the virtues develop, indirectly, naturally, spontaneously. Within those who abide in Christ the Spirit produces *the* fruit, the love which includes all the virtues.

Fruit through sacrifice

This love is dyed deep-red with the blood of Christ. The way to Pentecost is via Calvary. The fruit of the Spirit is the outcome of the sacrifice of Christ. As illustrations of this principle of fruitfulness through sacrifice, look in turn at a fruit, a seed and a tree. What is a fruit? It is in fact a seed box by which a tree reproduces itself. Inside a plum or a cherry is a seed; inside a grape or an apple there are a number of seeds. The fruit exists for the seed which it nourishes, protects and sometimes helps to distribute. It gives itself up for the production of new life.

Just before his passion and death Jesus likened himself to a grain of wheat. Cast into the soil, it dies – not literally but figuratively. While retaining the power of germination, it is completely transformed. As a seed it dies. It loses its identity and disintegrates. The food stored in the grain is used up to nourish the tiny embryo. Out of the disintegration of the seed the new life emerges. 'Truly, truly, I say to you, unless a grain of wheat falls into the earth and dies, it remains alone; but if it dies, it bears much fruit' (Jn. 12:24). Life, for others, comes through the death of Jesus; he bears fruit, countless lives redeemed, through his sacrifice. Had he saved his life he would have remained alone. He gave himself up on the cross and he was raised to life as the firstfruits of a great harvest. 'I, when I am lifted up from the earth, will draw all men to myself' (Jn. 12:32). After his sufferings, the Servant of the Lord 'exalted and lifted up…shall see the fruit of the travail of his soul and be satisfied' (Is. 52:13; 53:11).

The cross of Christ is the tree of life. The vertical and horizontal beams of the cross on which Christ hung were cut and shaped out of a tree or trees. To emphasize the element of shame and criminality both Peter and Paul refer to the cross – the scaffold, the gallows, the gibbet – as 'the tree' (Acts 10:39; 13:29; 1 Pet. 2:24). That tree of death was transformed by Christ into the tree of life. In God's new order, the prophet Ezekiel saw avenues of trees growing along the banks of a river which issued from the temple. 'On each bank of the stream all kinds of trees will grow to provide food. Their leaves will never wither, and they will never stop bearing fruit. They will have fresh fruit every month, because they are watered by the stream that flows from the Temple. The trees will provide food, and their leaves will be used for healing people' (Ezk. 47:12 GNB). In the middle of the Garden of Eden stood the tree of life (Gn. 2:9). In paradise restored John on Patmos saw that same tree, but, influenced by Ezekiel's vision, he used the expression collectively for the avenues of trees on either side of the river of life. The leaves of the tree of life have healing properties and its fruit is constant, varied and abundant (Rev. 22:2). In God's new creation the cross of Christ is the tree of life, symbol of immortality. Through the death and resurrection of Jesus men and nations are healed, nourished and restored to life eternal. Lives without number, saved from sin and death and transformed by the Holy Spirit into his likeness, are the fruits of the sacrifice of Christ.

Faithful cross! above all other,
    One and only noble tree!
None in foliage, none in blossom,
    None in fruit thy peer may be;
Sweetest wood and sweetest iron!
    Sweetest weight is hung on thee.[5]

Notes for chapter one

1. Quoted by John Baillie in *A Diary of Readings* (O.U.P., 1955), Day 2.
2. William Temple, *Readings in St John's Gospel* (Macmillan, 1947), p. 253.
3. John Donne, *Devotions*.
4. William Temple, *op. cit.*, p. 252.
5. From Latin hymn, 'Sing, my tongue, the glorious battle' by V. Fortunatus, tr. J. M. Neale.

2 The character of Christ

The Spirit of Jesus

'The fruits of the Spirit are nothing other than the virtues of Christ.'[1] This dictum of the famous German theologian Friedrich Schleiermacher points us in the right direction. We must look at the character of Christ carefully, since the fruits of the Spirit are his virtues. But we must not look at Christ at the outset and then forget his portrait. At every stage of this study our exposition of the meaning of each of the nine fruits of the Spirit must refer back constantly to the character of Christ. From start to finish our eyes must be fixed on Jesus.

For us, in the Christian era, the Holy Spirit is 'the Spirit of Jesus' (Acts 16:7). The Spirit existed before his coming, but ever since that coming the Spirit is inseparable from, is defined by, and is stamped with the personality of Christ. The Spirit was present with the people of the old covenant, and was active in many and various ways. But he came fitfully and temporarily, he spoke and acted through a small minority of God's people selected for special tasks. The Spirit was not permanently mediated through any one person. It was not yet clear who he was, or even that he was a person at all. The new era of the Spirit began when Jesus was baptized in the river Jordan. There Jesus was anointed with the Holy Spirit and with power for his vocation as Messiah and Servant. This anointing, this descent of the Spirit upon him in his fulness, was not temporary but permanent. 'I saw the Spirit descend as a dove from heaven, and it *remained* on him'

(Jn. 1:32). From that time on the Spirit is 'the Spirit of Jesus'. He rests upon Jesus, he is mediated through Jesus, he is given by Jesus. Above all, he is defined by Jesus. As light is coloured by passing through a stained-glass window, so, from the baptism onwards, and especially after the baptism with blood, the Spirit is coloured with the personality of Jesus. The Spirit is 'clearly focused for the first time in Jesus of Nazareth. No longer is his presence diffused; it is sharply localised in Jesus. No longer is it ill-defined; it is marked with the lineaments of his character.'[2]

It is into the image and likeness of Christ, the man with this character and these virtues, that the Spirit of Jesus transforms us. What matters most in life is that this image and likeness should be restored in each one of us, and in all of us together. 'Call the world if you please "The vale of soul-making".'[3] God's concern in this world is with character and especially with the formation of Christlike character. Those who have responded to God's call have 'put on the new nature, which is being constantly renewed in the image of its creator' (Col. 3:10), and brought to know God. This transformation into the image of God, the likeness of the Lord Jesus Christ, has already begun. It is a continuing process and a glorious hope. 'We all, with unveiled face, beholding the glory of the Lord, are being changed into his likeness from one degree of glory to another; for this comes from the Lord who is the Spirit' (2 Cor. 3:18). The sculptor, Michelangelo, worked for two years on a huge and damaged block of carrara marble. He shaped it into the gigantic statue of David, a figure of superb beauty and strength. It is God's purpose that we 'should be shaped to the likeness of his Son'. It takes more than two years! But through the ceaseless activity of the Holy Spirit, we can become more and more like Jesus until we bear his perfect likeness in the world to come. We know what this means because we can already see the image, the likeness of Christ. His character is revealed in the letters and gospels of the New Testament. As he was then, he is now; the Jesus Christ of today is the same as the Jesus Christ of yesterday. It's the virtues of his character we see in the New Testament that the Spirit of Jesus produces as fruits in us today. Looking at him, we can see what we are meant to be.

The character of Christ in the epistles

Our knowledge of the character of Christ comes from the letters and the gospels: in that order, because most of the letters were written before the gospels. They supply the earliest evidence of what Jesus was like. Most of the thirteen letters of the apostle Paul refer either directly or allusively to the character of Christ. He appeals to his converts at Corinth 'by the meekness and gentleness of Christ', and prays that the hearts of the believers at Thessalonica may be directed to 'the steadfastness of Christ' (2 Cor. 10:1; 2 Thes. 3:5). The Christians at Ephesus will be living 'as Christ' lived, if they are kind to one another and tenderhearted; if they forgive one another and walk in love (Eph. 4:32; 5:1-2). To the Philippians he writes, 'The attitude you should have is the one that Christ Jesus had…he was humble and walked the path of obedience all the way to death' (Phil. 2:5, 8 GNB). The members of the church at Corinth are urged to give generously to the collection for the needy, on the ground that they know all about the generosity of Christ (2 Cor. 8-9). In one passage Paul cites seven of the virtues of Christ, and in the case of the seventh, appeals explicitly to his example. 'Then put on the garments that suit God's chosen people, his own, his beloved: compassion, kindness, humility, gentleness, patience. Be forbearing with one another, and forgiving, where any of you has cause for complaint: you must forgive *as the Lord* forgave you.' He then goes on to speak of the supreme virtue of Christ, love, which binds all together and completes the whole (Col. 3:12-14 NEB). With reference to that supreme virtue, in his famous description of the fifteen facets of love, Paul is simply painting a portrait of Christ (1 Cor. 13:4-7). The apostle Peter writes of the patience and meekness of Christ before his accusers. He has 'left you an example; it is for you to follow in his steps' (1 Pet. 2:21 NEB). References to the character of Christ in the letters are sometimes allusive and indirect. 'You should wrap yourselves in the garment of humility towards each other' (1 Pet. 5:5 NEB) may, for example, be a reference to the towel with which Jesus girded himself before washing the feet of his disciples. The author of the Epistle to the Hebrews is acquainted with the story of Christ in the garden of Gethsemane. He draws attention to his religious awe, to his total submission and obedience (Heb. 5:7-8). There are other glimpses of the character of Christ in the letters of the apostles. The references here given to his meekness, gentleness, steadfastness, kindness, tenderness, compassion, generosity, patience, forbearance, forgiveness, humility, obedience, reverence, submissiveness and love make it abundantly clear that the Christian missionaries, preachers and teachers were acquainted with the salient facts. They frequently made the known character of Christ the ground for their ethical appeals.

The gospel portraits

The gospels, Matthew, Mark, Luke and John, are four portraits of Christ. In them we have, not the occasional glimpses and fragmentary sketches of the letters, but a more ample knowledge of his character. In the gospels we may see him on every page. The writers go out of their way to tell us what Jesus was like. They are less concerned with other aspects of biography as we know it. Many attempts were made in the nineteenth century to provide a more or less complete and chronological account of the life of Jesus. As recorded preaching, the gospels do not supply material of that kind, nor do they provide a sufficient quantity of material for anything like a biography. Those so-called 'Lives' of Jesus owed more to the imagination of the biographers than to the four evangelists.

There is, however, sufficient material to depict the *character* of Jesus. Not that it's possible to give a characterization, that is an exhaustive description of his character as portrayed in the gospels. For the usual procedure of selecting what is typical and distinctive cannot in this case be followed. In a funeral oration, for example, it's customary to eulogize the virtues and specific achievements of the person departed. We can describe a character only in terms of that which is typical and distinctive. 'Character means, generally speaking, a distinguishing mark, and hence when applied to human beings it denotes those qualities or traits that distinguish them from other human beings.'[4] We soon run into difficulties, however, if we attempt to name the traits, qualities, virtues which distinguish Jesus from other human beings. The list becomes so long that nothing stands out. It could be said that love, love for God and love for people, was the characteristic virtue of Jesus. That's true, but it's not a characterization. For love, the supreme virtue, includes all the others. The fruits of the Spirit, for example, are all aspects of love. Can it be claimed, then, that love, joy, peace, patience, kindness, goodness, faithfulness, gentleness, self-control, are the characteristic virtues of Christ? Yes, but only if Paul's list is regarded as typical, not as complete or exhaustive. The list can be extended. For example, it doesn't include two of the three outstanding graces of Christian character, faith (as distinct from faithfulness) and hope. Faith in God, love for people, hope for the coming of the Kingdom, are indeed characteristic of Jesus; yet to concentrate even on 'these three' exclusively would be to leave out other important aspects of his character.

The predominant impression made by the character of Christ is that of *fulness*. When the apostle Paul writes of 'the fulness of Christ', he is using the expression both individually and corporately, of Christ and the church. Jesus is the Second Adam, the New Man; he is full-grown, complete, mature. This fulness, seen first in Jesus, is to be realized in the total Christ, the Body of which Christ is the head and 'we all' are the members (Eph. 4:13). Fulness in the fellowship comes from the fulness of Christ. Like the grace of God the character of Christ is also manifold, many-sided, many-coloured. It's like a diamond with a variety of beautiful facets or a rainbow compounded of many lovely colours. Rather than dissect his character or list his virtues it's better to look at the whole diamond, the many-coloured rainbow, the complete person.

In Jesus Christ we also find fulness of life and vigour,

amazing vitality. Here is one who is intensely alive. This vitality is to be seen in all three aspects of his personality: intellectual, emotional, volitional. His mind is swift and penetrating. Every attempt to catch him by craft or to defeat him in controversy is doomed to failure (Mk. 12:13-40). He thinks in vivid pictures, setting forth the truth with simplicity; yet men have never fathomed the amazing depth of his teaching. His emotional completeness and intensity are no less remarkable. For Jesus is no stoic cultivating apathy and stifling his emotions...he is moved with compassion at the sight of the leper; with fierce anger he drives the merchants from the temple courts. He sighs in sorrow, weeps in grief, rejoices in the Holy Spirit. There is a full flow of emotional life. When we turn to the virtues of his vocation we shall look at the strength of his firm and inflexible will. In what other human being do we find the full and equal development of these three aspects of personality?

Balance and excess

In the character of Christ there is unity and balance. A cut diamond has a variety of facets but it is one stone. The virtues of Christ are not found in isolation but in a complex whole. In the unity of his character each virtue is balanced by its opposite. That is unusual, for in most of us there are varying degrees of imbalance. Our virtues often have the defects of their qualities, for each one is not counter-balanced by its complement. Tolerance, for example, is a virtue, especially in a democratic society, but, as Edmund Burke observed, 'there is a limit at which forbearance ceases to be a virtue'. It can become an easy-going and spineless acquiescence in error or in evil. If a man is zealous and ambitious he is apt to be hard and intolerant; if, on the other hand, he is gentle and kindly, he may lack conviction and drive. Zeal can degenerate into violence, fervour into fanaticism, liberty into licence. The bold become reckless; the righteous, censorious; the gentle, 'meek and mild'. Over-grown virtues expel their complementaries, and the person becomes eccentric, that is, off-centre. The virtues of Christ are never thus isolated from their complementaries. Here are a few examples. Jesus was often moved with compassion; at other times he responded to people with warm indignation. The man of joy was also the man of sorrows. He could be both tranquil and disturbed, serene and agitated. While he acted and taught with complete assurance and authority, he served others with profound respect and humility. He loved society and he loved solitude. Intensely practical, he was also a man of prayer. The complementary traits are at times sharply contrasted and there is tension as well as harmony. Severe in his judgments, he was gentle in his relationships. Zeal for his cause and inflexible resolve did not destroy his calmness of mind and heart. Considerate and courteous, he could be frank and provocative. The Prince of Peace was a man of controversy. His vision of and commitment to the grand plan and purpose of God went hand in hand with a sensitive awareness of and deep concern for the needs of apparently insignificant individuals. The man for others was strongly self-assertive. In a word, there is in Jesus a perfect balance of character. He is complete.

Balance, however, does not mean moderation. The character of Christ does not correspond to the portrait of the perfect man as painted by Aristotle. The Greek philosopher is concerned with 'the golden mean'. Each virtue is midway between two extremes, the extreme of defect and the extreme of excess. There is a happy medium. Take, for example, the cardinal virtue of temperance. It is possible to eat or drink too little, or too much. For all the virtues the Greek ideal is the middle way, the avoidance of extremes, 'nothing too much'. Such a well-rounded character, sober and cautious, having all the virtues in due moderation and proportion, has nothing in common with the character of Christ. His brothers didn't go down to Capernaum to arrest Jesus because he was an all-rounder of that kind. 'They set out to take charge of him, because people were saying, "He's gone mad!"' (Mk. 3:21 GNB). In his singleness of purpose, his burning zeal, his total commitment to his mission, he was regarded by some as a misguided and unbalanced fanatic. Similarly, Jesus required of his disciples a complete devotion, a total commitment, not the virtue of 'the mean' but the virtue of the extreme. 'Jesus teaches an excess in virtue, an excess in forbearance, an excess in gentleness, an excess in giving and yielding. Virtue, the full virtue of a disciple, is an excess, a full devotion, an overflowing measure.'[5] Jesus was delighted when he found the virtues of faith and love, of forbearance and forgiveness, of goodwill and generosity, in an *extreme* form. If we do only what can be reasonably and convention-ally expected of us, 'what is there extraordinary about that?' It is the *extra*-ordinary that Jesus requires, goodness without limit (Mt. 5:47-48 NEB). When a virtue is counterbalanced by other virtues it may, without defect or distortion, be exercised to excess. It is possible and desirable to have virtues in excess, and to 'complete a balanced character that will fall short in nothing' (Jas. 1:4 NEB).

His filial virtues

There is no direct description anywhere in the gospels of the virtues of Jesus. They are revealed to us indirectly in his words and deeds, his attitudes and his relationships. We can best study his virtues in connection with the two great commandments he gave to us, his summary of the law and the prophets. Jesus loved God and Jesus loved people. Together with his attitudes to God and to men, we shall also look at his attitude to his work, the virtues of his vocation.

The attitude of Jesus to God is characterized by reverence, obedience and trust. He was vividly aware of the living God, the holy One, and responded to him with the reverence and awe due from a son. 'During his life on earth, he offered up prayer and entreaty, aloud and in silent tears, to the one who had the power to save him out of death' (Heb. 5:7 JB). His prayers were heard 'because of his religious awe' (*eulabeia*)…because he had God in reverence'. In his own prayers and in the prayer he taught his disciples, reverence is linked with obedience. His prayer in Gethsemane was heard and answered because it was a prayer of total submission to the will of God. 'Abba (Father)!' he said. 'Everything is possible for you. Take this cup away from me. But let it be as you, not I, would have it' (Mk. 14:36 JB). Reverence for God and obedience to his will are also linked in the Lord's Prayer, 'May your name be held holy…your will be done.' God's nature revealed is to be held in awe, and his will is to be done on earth as in heaven. On one occasion, when his disciples offered him food, Jesus claimed that obedience to the will of God was his refreshment and sustenance. 'My food…is to obey the will of the one who sent me and to finish the work he gave me to do' (Jn. 4:34 GNB). Obedience was not easy or automatic for Jesus. It came through strife; he had to learn obedience in the school of suffering. The submission he offered to God throughout the whole course of his life was consummated in the sacrifice of perfect obedience (Heb. 5:8; 10:5-10). 'He was humble and walked the path of obedience all the way to death – his death on the cross' (Phil. 2:8 GNB).

Jesus was enabled to obey because he completely trusted God and entirely entrusted his life to God. This trustfulness is to be seen in his prayers, in his deeds and in the whole course of his ministry. In his prayers Jesus habitually addressed God as *Abba*. This was the intimate Aramaic term for *father*, used by the children of that time. The relationship between the Son and the Father was a relationship of intimacy and trust. His trustfulness was evident in his work as well as in his prayers. It took the form of a complete dependence on God. As an apprentice carpenter Jesus had learned the trade by watching Joseph at work and by doing what his 'father' did. As *the* Son of *the* Father he does only what he sees the Father doing. 'For the Father loves the Son and shows him all that he himself is doing…the Son can do nothing on his own; he does only what he sees his Father doing' (Jn. 5:20, 19). The works of Jesus were the works of God, done through him, by him. What is more, Jesus believed that the whole course and the consummation of his ministry had been chartered and ordained by God (Lk. 13:32-33). This enabled him throughout his ministry to maintain an attitude of complete trust in God and in the hour of death to commit himself and his work trustfully into the hands of his Father (Lk.23:46)..

The virtues of the Son due to the Father are reverence,

obedience and trust. These three are the components of love. For to love God is to fear him, to obey him, to trust him. In the Old Testament reverence and obedience were regarded as components of love. To love the Lord is to fear him and to keep his commandments (Dt. 10:12-13). But whereas awe, as a component of love, is predominant in the Old Covenant, trust is the more prominent in the New Covenant. In Jesus Christ we find all three components of love in perfection. He, and he alone, fulfilled the first and great commandment by revering, obeying and trusting God with all his heart, soul, mind and strength.

The virtues of his vocation

The character and the vocation of Christ belong together. In this respect he is no exception. In all great men, character and cause, what a man is and what he lives for, are as inseparable as the warp and woof of a garment. For character is not created and shaped in a vacuum; it is educed and developed by the purpose for which a man lives, by the cause for which he stands. Jesus is what he does and does what he is. He is 'the anointed one', the Christ; but he is anointed by the Holy Spirit for the exercise and fulfilment of his vocation as Servant and Messiah, as Saviour and King (Lk. 4:18-19). He came to fulfil God's purpose for Israel, revealed in the law and the prophets. That purpose was the coming of the Kingdom, the establishment of God's reign on earth. Present in the person and mission of Jesus, the Kingdom had come already; it would be established with power. It was in his commitment to this cause of God that the virtues of his vocation were revealed.

Faithfulness, the seventh in Paul's list of the fruits of the Spirit, is the outstanding virtue of Christ's vocation, and will be dealt with fully in chapter ten. Jesus also taught and exemplified the need for *single-mindedness* in the service of God, a virtue which is itself akin to purity and sincerity, to zeal and enthusiasm. Jesus the teacher commends the single eye and the single service. If the eye is healthy the whole body will be full of light. Illumination depends on simplicity, vision on singleness of intention. Happy is the man who is single-minded, who has one steady aim, who gives a single service to one Master. 'No servant can be a slave of two masters.' The genuine disciple is a man of undivided allegiance; he gives absolute priority to the cause of God. 'Set your mind on God's kingdom and his justice before everything else' (Mt. 6:33 NEB). This simplicity of intention is related to the virtues of purity and sincerity. The pure is that which is unmixed, unadulterated. Purity of heart is to will one thing and upon this simplicity, as distinct from duplicity of intention, depends the vision of God (Mt. 5:8). Sincerity is freedom from falsehood and hypocrisy. Almsgiving, prayer and fasting must be free from ulterior motives. The sincere man has a single motive – the intention to please God in all his actions (Mt. 6:1-18). Zeal is single-minded devotion to a cause, and enthusiasm is the warmth and ardour with which it is pursued and advanced. The former has reference primarily to the will, and the latter to the emotions. All these virtues – purity, sincerity, zeal, enthusiasm – Jesus required of his disciples. They are components of the single-mindedness, the whole-heartedness of Jesus himself who with one mind and heart devoted himself to his vocation. This virtue has been called Christ's choicest gift to his disciples.

> Hear us, Lord, and that right soon;
> Hear, and grant the choicest boon
> That Thy love can e'er impart,
> Loyal singleness of heart.[6]

The virtue of courage was exhibited by Jesus throughout his ministry and supremely in his passion and death. Although the word for courage (*andreia* – one of the four cardinal virtues of the Greeks) is not used by Jesus or of him, the quality itself is to be seen in full strength in his character and conduct. It is not an independent virtue; it is the habitual disposition of mind with which Jesus faced the challenges and hazards of his vocation. He was bold in speech. 'In the records of his life we have pages upon pages of controversy. It may have been

41

far from the work in which he delighted most to be engaged; but he had to undertake it all through his life, and especially towards its close.'[7] Jesus was a doughty controversialist who did not pull his punches. 'Teacher, we know that you tell the truth, without worrying about what people think' (Mk. 12:14 GNB). His forthright words provoked opposition and made enemies (Mk.3:6). As in utterances, so also in action, Jesus was fearlessly aggressive and pugnacious. To drive the traders and money-changers out of the courtyard of the temple was an act of superb courage. It made the hierarchs he had challenged determined to kill him (Mk. 11:15-19). Jesus manifested all four kinds of courage, physical and moral courage, and the courage to do and to endure. His passion was both active and passive, a doing and an enduring. With courage, both physical and moral, at full strength he confronted and triumphed over hostility and abuse, shame and suffering. In this way he became the exemplar and inspirer of all the heroes of faith (Heb. 12:2).

The virtues of his personal relationships

Some of the virtues of Jesus are exhibited in his personal relationships. From his many social virtues we select three that are outstanding, his *affection* for his friends, his *compassion* for the needy, his *forgiveness* for his enemies.

Jesus loved all his fellow-men. Within that large circle was a smaller circle. John refers to this in his introduction to the passion story. 'He had always loved his own who were in the world, and now he was to show the full extent of his love' (Jn. 13:1 NEB). Even within that circle of 'his own' there were smaller circles. Soon after his resurrection, the Lord Jesus had 'more than five hundred' disciples (1 Cor. 15:6). Within that outer circle was the inner circle of the twelve, and within the twelve there was the innermost circle of Peter, James and John, and among the three there was John, 'the disciple whom Jesus loved'. Jesus loved his own with intensity, with emotional warmth. His love for this small group was affectionate, like the warm-hearted love between the parents and children, the brothers and sisters of a good family. They

42

were his parents, his brothers and sisters, his family (Mk. 3:33-35). His love for his own was also friendship-love. 'No longer do I call you servants, for the servant does not know what his master is doing; but I have called you friends, for all that I have heard from my Father I have made known to you' (Jn. 15:15). Friendship is here defined in terms of confiding. A servant does not know his master's secrets. The disciples are friends of Jesus because he has confided in them the secrets of the Kingdom of God and the truth about his own person and mission. In his essay on *Friendship,* Ralph Emerson writes, 'There are two elements that go to the composition of friendship – truth and tenderness.' The relationship of Jesus to his own was one of truth. He did not hide, he revealed himself; he was not secretive but open. He was frank and transparent. But truth would be cold and hard without tenderness. There was warmth as well as light. The disciples were dear to Jesus, his chosen were his beloved. His overflowing tenderness of heart, his affectionate love was lavished upon his true family. To them and for them, in his sufferings and sacrifice, he showed the full extent of his love; he laid down his life for his friends.

There are many references in the gospels to the compassion of Jesus. During his ministry he was constantly confronted with human need. The lepers and the blind cried out for mercy (Lk. 17:13; Mt. 20:30). 'When he saw the crowds, he had compassion for them, because they were harassed and helpless, like sheep without a shepherd' (Mt. 9:36). His heart went out to a widow bereaved of her only son (Lk. 7:13). Sorry for a weary and hungry multitude, he fed them all (Mk. 8:2). With few exceptions, his mighty deeds were works of mercy; he was motivated by compassion. The mercy of Jesus was an inner feeling, a mighty stirring within the heart of emotions warm and tender. He was moved to the depths of his being. The compassion of Jesus, however, did not remain in the realm of feeling – he was *moved* by compassion to action. The inner gave rise to the outer, depth of feeling to act of succour. He healed the sick, cleansed the leper, taught the ignorant, fed the hungry, restored the outcast, delivered the oppressed. Such compassion was costly. Sympathy is feeling with; compassion is suffering with. 'He took away our ill-nesses and bore the burden of our diseases' (Mt. 8:17 NEB margin). The words of the prophet, applied to the healing ministry of Jesus by the evangelist, point also to the climax of that ministry. His compassion led him to the cross.

'The Son of Man has authority on earth to forgive sins' (Mk. 2:10 GNB). As the agent of God, Jesus both declared and mediated the divine forgiveness. Like a doctor among the sick, Jesus kept company with sinners. He sought them out, called them, sat at table with them, welcomed them into the fellowship of God. His attitudes and relationships exhibited and conveyed the reality which his words announced. From the forgiven, he accepted, as God's representative, the reverence, adoration and gratitude due only to God (Lk. 7:40-50). The forgiveness he proclaimed and offered was without limit. When he was crucified, he prayed, 'Father, forgive them; for they know not what they do' (Lk. 23:34). The forgiveness he preached and practised he required of his disciples. Having received unlimited forgiveness from God, they in turn must offer unlimited forgiveness to others (Mt. 18:21-35). Paul has in mind the ministry and passion of Christ when he writes, 'You must forgive one another just as the Lord has forgiven you' (Col. 3:13 GNB).

Virtues are attitudes. The attitude of Christ to his friends was affectionate, and to those who were in need, compassion-ate. To his enemies and to all sinners who repent he declares and reveals, embodies and offers the forgiveness of God.

The example of Christ

To make us like Christ in character is the work of the Holy Spirit. If we are to work with him in that task then we must know what Christ was like. We must have the exemplar before our eyes if we are to follow his example. There can be no genuine imitation of Christ apart from a historical knowledge of him. This is a defect in that otherwise superb devotional classic *The Imitation of Christ* by Thomas à Kempis. 'No painter could make a satisfactory copy of a figure of which he had himself only a vague conception. Yet no exact image of Christ will be found in à Kempis. To him Christ is the union and sum of all possible excellences; but he constructs Christ out of his own notions of excellence, instead of going to the records of his life and painting the portrait with the colours they supply.'[8]

Within those records, we are taught and exhorted to follow the example of Jesus Christ. We are to serve others with humility *as Christ* served us (Mk. 10:43-45). After he had washed the feet of his disciples, Jesus said, 'I have given you an example, that you also should do as I have done to you' (Jn. 13:15). Stephen, the first martyr, deliberately followed the example of his Lord's magnanimity; he died praying that his enemies might be forgiven (Acts 7:60). The attitude of Christians to one another is to be modelled on that of Christ. He didn't grasp at equality, he emptied himself; he took the form of a servant, he humbled himself becoming obedient unto death (Phil. 2:5-8). 'Be kind to one another, tender-hearted, forgiving one another, *as God in Christ* forgave you. Therefore be imitators of God, as beloved children. And walk in love, *as Christ* loved us and gave himself up for us, a fragrant offering and sacrifice to God' (Eph. 4:32-5:2). The passion of Christ is held forth as an example for Christians. Slaves are urged to accept injustice and beatings with patient endurance – like Jesus, who did not retaliate when he was unjustly insulted, beaten and crucified. 'For to this you have been called, because Christ also suffered for you, leaving you an example (*hypogrammos*), that you should follow in his steps' (1 Pet. 2:21).

These direct, and other indirect, references in the New Testament set forth the life and death of Jesus Christ as an example which Christians are to follow. Not that we are called to imitate the externals and accidentals of the character and conduct of Jesus. 'He is not an optimal model simply to be copied in every detail, but a basic model to be realized in an infinite variety of ways according to time, place and person.'[9] It is the mind that was in Christ Jesus, his basic attitudes towards God, towards his calling, towards people, that the Spirit seeks to reproduce in his disciples.

Plato tells us in the *Protagoras* how a Greek boy was taught to write. Across his wax tablet the schoolmaster drew parallel lines to keep the boy's writing straight, and on the top line he wrote a sentence which the boy was to copy out on the lines below. That top line of perfect script was called the *hypogrammos*. 'Just as the school-boy learns to write by copying the perfect copper-plate example, so we are scholars in the school of life, and we can only learn to live by copying the perfect pattern of life which Jesus gave to us.'[10] The one who helps and enables us to do this is the Holy Spirit. We co-operate by fixing our eyes upon Jesus and by following in his steps.

Notes for chapter two

1. F. D. E. Schleiermacher (1768-1834), *Der Christliche Glaube*, II, par. 125.
2. Michael Green, *I believe in the Holy Spirit* (Hodder and Stoughton, 1975), p.51.
3. John Keats.
4. J. N. Lapsley, *A Dictionary of Christian Ethics*, ed. J. Macquarrie (S.C.M., 1967), p.51.
5. C. G. Montefiore, *Rabbinic Literature and Gospel Teachings* (Macmillan, 1930), p.52.
6. From the hymn, 'At Thy feet, O Christ, we lay' by William Bright.
7. James Stalker, *Imago Christi* (Hodder and Stoughton, 1889), pp.285-286.
8. James Stalker, *ibid.*, p.29.
9. Hans Küng, *On Being a Christian* (Collins, 1977), p.551.
10. William Barclay, *New Testament Wordbook* (S.C.M., 1955), pp. 55-56.

3 Fruits and gifts

Things that differ

So far, our concern has been Christian character, the fruits of
the Spirit, the virtues of Christ. We now go on to look at the
fruits and the gifts of the Spirit and to study the relationship
between them. The fruits and the gifts of the Spirit are alike
in one respect; both come from the Spirit. But they are not
the same; there is a basic difference between them. The fruits
of the Spirit are the virtues he produces in the character of a
Christian. The gifts of the Spirit are the abilities entrusted to
the Christian. Fruits have to do with character, gifts with
service. The fruits are a description of what a Christian is
meant to *be;* the gifts are indicative of what a Christian is
meant to *do*.

Unfortunately it is possible to have the aptitudes without
the qualities, the gifts without the graces. Samson, for
example, was endowed by the Spirit with great physical
strength. He destroyed a lion, slew thirty men and burst the
ropes that bound him. All the same, his character was ruined
by undisciplined temper and sex. He had the gift of might; he
lacked the fruit of self-control. Solomon was famed for his
wisdom, a gift of the Spirit. But his character was far from
admirable. His extravagance, sensuality and tyranny were
responsible for the impoverishment, corruption and disruption of the kingdom. As in the Old, so in the New Testament. The gifted are not necessarily the good. Some of those
who have exercised the gifts of prophecy, exorcism and the
working of miracles will, on grounds of character, be

condemned at the Last Judgment. The ability to say and to do wonderful things is not accepted as a substitute for obedience (Mt. 7:21-23). A man may be both a gifted speaker and a bad character. The gifted healer may be mercenary; the talented singer conceited and ambitious. Gifts are no index to character; ability is no sign of holiness. Apart from good character, gifts are at best useless; they can be harmful and destructive.

There is a simple way of distinguishing fruits and gifts, virtues and abilities. It is the distinction between *all* and *some*. The fruits of the Spirit, being qualities of character, are for all Christians. They are indispensable. Love, for example, 'without which whoever lives is counted dead', is not for some Christians only. It is essential for all. So, too, Christians without joy or peace would be sub-normal. To be without kindness or patience, goodness or fidelity, would be a grave deficiency in any Christian. Gentleness is not optional and a believer without self-control would be like an ancient city without defensive walls. In short, there is not one of the nine fruits which is not intended for every Christian. On the other hand, no Christian has, or is intended to have, all the gifts of the Spirit. 'Are all apostles? Are all prophets? Are all teachers?' Within the Christian community there are relatively few apostles, prophets, teachers, preachers, pastors, missionaries, evangelists. A few are gifted for these functions, most are not. 'Do all work miracles? Do all possess gifts of healing? Do all speak with tongues? Do all interpret?' The implied answer to this series of rhetorical questions is obvious. Not all. Some have this gift, some that, some the other (1 Cor. 12:29-30). 'If the whole body were an eye, where would be the hearing? If the whole body were an ear, where would be the sense of smell?' (1 Cor. 12:17). In the church, the body of Christ, each member has a different but indispensable function. Different gifts are entrusted to different people, according to the sovereign will of God. The gifts vary from one another. The fruits are, or should be, common to all.

This distinction between fruits and gifts is not meant to imply that the fruits are not also, if in a quite different sense, gifts. For the virtues of Christ are also given to Christians. They are not manufactured by us; they are produced by the Spirit. They are fruit; they are not achievements. In that sense, fruits are gifts, qualities given. So theologians and writers sometimes refer to the fruits of the Spirit as gifts. This leads to confusion because the word *gift* is ambiguous. It can be used in two ways, of a quality given, or of a special ability given. In the first sense the fruits of the Spirit are gifts; in the second sense they are not. They are qualities of character, virtues of Christ, fruits of the Spirit; they are not *charismata*. To avoid confusion, we shall call the qualities of character given by the Spirit, virtues, graces, fruits; and the special endowments given by the Spirit for the performance of special tasks, gifts, abilities, *charismata*.

The gifts

Fruits and gifts, then, are to be distinguished. They should not be divorced; nor should they be set in antithesis. They are not alternatives between which believers must choose. It is a mistake to try to enhance the virtues by devaluing the gifts. Some Christians do this. They maintain that what really matters in the Christian life is the fruits, not the gifts, of the Spirit. In fact, they both matter. It is not a case of either-or but of both-and. A gift (*charisma*) is a special endowment for the performance of a special task on behalf of the people of God. In the New Testament there are seven lists of these gifts.

The apostle Peter mentions two general activities only; speaking and serving, the ministry of the Word and practical ministry (1 Pet. 4:10-11). The apostle Paul gives three lists in chapter 12 of 1 Corinthians. Nine gifts are cited in verses 8 to 10, the utterance of wisdom, the utterance of knowledge, faith, gifts of healing, the working of miracles, prophecy, the ability to distinguish between spirits, various kinds of tongues, the interpretation of tongues. Five of these gifts are mentioned again in the lists at the end of the same chapter and four new ones appear. 'And God has appointed in the church first apostles, second prophets, third teachers, then workers of miracles, then healers, helpers, administrators, speakers in various kinds of tongues.' In the third list, after repeating six of the eight gifts just cited, he adds the gift of interpreting tongues (1 Cor. 12:28-30). In the next chapter Paul selects six gifts to illustrate his point that no gift is of any value without love: tongues, prophecy, knowledge, faith, almsgiving, martyrdom (1 Cor. 13:1-3). Paul mentions seven gifts in Romans chapter 12, prophecy, service, teaching, exhortation, giving to charity, leadership, helping those in distress. The gifts in this list are more easily described in terms of the person exercising the gift, the prophet, the administrator, the teacher, the encourager, the almsgiver, the leader, the doer of kindness (Rom. 12:6-8). This applies also to the later list of four gifts in Ephesians chapter 4. 'And his gifts were that some should be apostles, some prophets, some evangelists, some pastors and teachers' (Eph. 4:11). In examining these seven lists we note that some of the gifts appear a number of times. Allowing for these repetitions some twenty gifts of the Spirit are found in these lists or elsewhere in the New Testament. No two lists are the same. From this it may be inferred that the lists of gifts are intended to be illustrative and typical. The apostles are not saying, 'these are the gifts of the Spirit, no more, no less'. 'At least twenty (gifts) are specified in the New Testament, and the living God who loves variety and is a generous giver may well bestow many, many more than that.'[1] He has in fact done so. Just as there are not nine virtues of Christ and no more, so there are not nine gifts of the Spirit, or twenty, and no more.

Natural and supernatural

God is both Creator and Redeemer. For a right understanding of the fruits and gifts of the Holy Spirit it is of vital importance to keep that in mind. To lose sight of that basic truth is to fall into error. One way of divorcing the work of God the Creator from the work of God the Redeemer is to make a distinction and a contrast between the natural and the supernatural, and then to confine the work of the Spirit to the latter realm. This false contrast can be applied both to the fruits and to the gifts. There are, it would seem, certain virtues which are natural to man, apart from the new life in Christ. Courage, fairness, kindness, for example, while not found in all men, are to be seen in good men everywhere in all ages. On the other hand, it is said, the supernatural virtues of faith, love and hope belong to believers only. Some gifts, it is observed, belong to men by birth and may be developed by education and training. A person doesn't have to be a Christian to be a gifted singer, mechanic, doctor or administrator. On the other hand, so it is claimed, speaking with tongues, prophecy and the like, are supernatural gifts.

We misinterpret the Bible if we read back into it distinctions made in subsequent ages which were not in the minds of the biblical authors themselves. One such distinction is the contrast between the natural and the supernatural. Since the Renaissance the term *nature* has been used by naturalists to denote the entire universe, excluding the possibility of anything other than or beyond nature. In this sense nature is self-sufficient, a fixed order, a system of cause and effect, within which all things and events are interlocked, an independent and self-explanatory process. Nature exists and continues on its own. Given this conception of nature, those who reject it are compelled to make a distinction between nature and that which is super-nature, *i.e.* above and beyond it. Not having been confronted with such a conception of nature, the biblical authors were under no such compulsion. There is no word equivalent to our word *nature* in Hebrew, nor is the naturalist's concept of nature to be found in the Hebrew mind. The biblical writers were certainly aware of sequences, regularity and order in the world: but these are regarded as given, maintained and guaranteed by God (Gn. 8:22). The world comes from him, is maintained by him, is dependent on him and is the sphere of his activity. It is everywhere and at all times open to his presence and creative power. He is transcendent and immanent; he is underneath and above, behind and beyond the world, in which he is present and active.

Confusion is worse confounded if, having made a distinction between the natural and the supernatural, we then seek to limit and confine the work of the Holy Spirit to

51

the latter realm. 'I believe in the Holy Spirit in the holy Church' (Hippolytus). That indeed is the special sphere of his operation. But he is not confined to it. 'The wind blows where it wills' (Jn. 3:8). 'Just as it is impossible to control the wind or dictate to it its direction, so no man, no church, can domesticate the Spirit of God or delimit his sphere of operation.'[2] He is the Creator Spirit.

> Darkness profound
> Cover'd the abyss; but on the watery calm
> His brooding wings the Spirit of God outspread,
> And vital virtue infus'd, and vital warmth,
> Throughout the fluid mass.[3]

The Spirit is God in action, creating and giving life to all things (Pss. 33:6; 104:30). The Word, the Wisdom, the Spirit of God are in the Old Testament, three different ways of expressing God's presence and activity within his creation, inanimate, animate and human. All life and light, all goodness and ability come from him. The Spirit is the one source of every virtue and every gift, wherever, whenever and in whomsoever found.

> All the lamps that guide the world
> Were kindled at thy flame.[4]

Love transforms the virtues

So the virtues of the natural man are the creation of the Spirit of God. At all times and in all places men have been aware of the moral law. Men can distinguish right from wrong; all have an innate awareness that one ought to do this and ought not to do that. Moral standards may vary from age to age and from place to place, but that does not alter the basic fact that all men are aware of the difference between right and wrong, and of the obligation to do the right and refuse the wrong. Paul affirms this of all men. 'The Gentiles do not have the (Mosaic) Law; but whenever they do by instinct what the Law commands, they are their own law, even though they do not have the Law. Their conduct shows that what the Law commands is written in their hearts. Their consciences also show that this is true, since their thoughts sometimes accuse them and sometimes defend them' (Rom. 2:14-15 GNB). All men are aware of the moral law within; some men have sincerely endeavoured to obey it. 'For in all ages there have been some persons, who, from the mere dictates of nature, have devoted their whole lives to the pursuit of virtue.'[5]

Let us look at one selection from the virtues of character recognized by decent and civilized people everywhere. According to the Greek philosopher Plato, there are four cardinal virtues, prudence, justice, temperance, fortitude. *Prudence* or wisdom is common sense, practical sagacity. The wise man thinks in advance, foresees the possible outcome of his actions and thus makes a shrewd choice of the line of conduct to be pursued. *Justice* has reference to the dealings of the individual with others. It includes honesty and truthfulness, the keeping of promises, the fulfilment of contracts, the faithful discharge of every duty and social obligation. *Temperance* has to do with the pleasures of life. The temperate man is orderly; he accepts and he resists. He is able to go the right length in enjoying the pleasures of life and he is able to resist the temptation to go to excess. *Fortitude* or courage is both active and passive; it includes both valour and endurance. It's the manliness which can face fear and danger and which can bear trials and sufferings with patience. These are splendid virtues, but they can become splendid vices! For the natural man is a sinner and his virtues are always tainted and are often corrupted by sin. The virtues of the natural man are inherently man-centred; they are not created and developed by response to God or concern for the neighbour. Sin is self-centredness; it corrupts the virtues with egoism. Sin is self-righteousness; the virtuous man becomes proud of his virtues and seeks to justify himself on that ground, before men and before God. So the virtuous man stands in need of redemption and his virtues need to be cleansed, re-directed and transformed.

Since the Middle Ages Christian character has been described in terms of the seven virtues, the four cardinal virtues and the three theological virtues. Thomas Aquinas took over the four cardinal virtues from Plato and Aristotle and related them to the three theological virtues, the Christian triad of graces, faith, hope and love. *Faith* is man's response to the event of Jesus Christ, to his ministry, death and resurrection. To have faith is to trust and entrust our lives to the God who encounters us in Christ incarnate, crucified and risen. *Hope*, like faith, is a response to the activity of God in Christ. It is desire with expectation, and has reference to God's activity in the future. The work which God has begun in Christ we desire and expect him to continue in this life and to complete in the world to come. *Love* is the very nature of the eternal God, manifested in the life and sacrifice of Jesus Christ, and operating in us by the Holy Spirit. The three graces are inter-dependent, but love is greater than faith and hope (1 Cor. 13:13). The active love of God in Christ is the reality to which faith responds; it is also the ground and the goal of Christian hope. When the natural virtues are brought into this new dimension, when they are related to the love which includes faith and hope, then they are rescued from the service of self and wedded to the service of God and our fellow-men.

The love which believes all things and hopes all things unifies, transforms and directs the natural virtues. Love unifies; the virtues are no longer plural, separate and un-related, developing unevenly. In the service of love they are bound together. Love transforms and re-directs. There is a change of centre, from self to God and the neighbour. Liberated from the service of the self, they are transformed through re-direction; they become Christ-centred and other people-centred. There is a change of master. The virtues are under the control of love. The natural is not destroyed; it is fulfilled in love. This may be illustrated from each of the four cardinal virtues. They are christianized. Jesus makes a contrast between a rogue, praised, not for his dishonesty but for his *prudence*, and 'the sons of light' who all too often act without foresight and shrewdness. Prudence in the service of self can be transformed by love into prudence in the service of God and man. There is no opposition between love and dealing justly with others; there can be a denial of love in demanding *justice* from others. To Shylock demanding his pound of flesh, no more, no less, Portia said:

> Therefore, Jew,
> Though justice be thy plea, consider this,
> That in the course of justice none of us
> Should see salvation.[6]

By going beyond the legitimate claims of others upon us, and by setting aside our legitimate claims upon others, justice is fulfilled by love. When *temperance* is christianized it is no longer the control of the self in the interests of the self; it is the self controlled for the sake of others. So too, when *fortitude* is baptized into Christ, then fear and danger are faced and trials and sufferings are borne for the sake of the neighbour and of Christ. What is said of the four cardinal virtues could be extended to all the virtues of the natural man. That which the Spirit created originally he does not destroy; he takes it up into the new creation, the dimension of grace. The work of God the Creator is continued and fulfilled in the work of God the Redeemer and God the Sanctifier.

Love controls the gifts

As with the virtues, so with the gifts: we must not divorce the work of God as Creator and as Redeemer. There are gifts of nature and there are gifts of grace. It is obvious that a person doesn't have to be a Christian in order to be gifted. People are born with gifts, aptitudes, talents. These abilities can usually be developed by education and training. They can be strengthened and increased by use. They atrophy through disuse; like the limbs of the body, if we don't use them, we lose them. We recognize the existence of these natural gifts in the expressions we use. John, we say, is 'a born athlete' and Joan 'has music in her blood'. Mark simply loves tinkering with machines and Carol takes to languages like a duck to water. Margaret is good at teaching and Mary has a gift for administration. David has innate artistic abilities and Peter

55

has the gift of eloquence. That which is potential can become actual; gifts can be developed because they are already there. Otherwise no amount of practice would produce the gifted singer, speaker or leader. Even a man's temperament can be a gift. While Roy is naturally shy and reserved his wife Helen is by nature 'a good mixer' and gets on well with strangers. To call an ability natural is not to deny that it is a gift. The word *gift* presupposes a giver. Natural abilities are the gifts of the Creator Spirit to man as man.

How are these natural gifts related to the grace-gifts, the *charismata* listed in the New Testament? We must be careful at this juncture not to bring back the discarded distinction between the natural and the supernatural. There is a valid distinction between the old and the new creation, between the natural man and 'a man in Christ' (2 Cor. 12:2). In Christ, in accordance with the sovereign will of God, a person may be entrusted with one or more of the *charismata*. These grace-gifts, however, are related to that person's natural abilities, since the Pentecostal Spirit is also the Creator Spirit. 'May barrenness rejoice to own Thy fertilizing power.'[7] The Spirit is like water transforming the desert into paradise. 'For I will pour water on the thirsty land…I will pour my Spirit upon your descendants, and my blessing on your offspring. They shall spring up like grass amid waters, like willows by flowing streams' (Is. 44:3-4). Though barren, the land is alive and responds to the rain. In human life, the Spirit fertilizes what is already present, making it productive and fruitful. When we surrender to Christ our natural aptitudes the Spirit purifies and strengthens, enriches and intensifies them. This does not mean that the Spirit imparts no new or additional gifts to the man in Christ. He may; he often does. But 'his spiritual gifts dovetail with his natural endowments'.[8] The latter are transformed and transfigured by grace. 'We therefore see both our initial genetic constitution and our subsequent spiritual endowments as sovereignly given and perfectly fitted together.'[9]

The love which transforms the virtues also controls the gifts. Love is regulatory. In God's intention the exercise of the gifts should always be under the control of love. It is at this point that the inherent relationship between the fruits and the gifts of the Spirit is most clearly seen. For the love which regulates includes within itself all the fruits of the Spirit. It is love as joy, love as peace, love as patience, *etc.* Taking some of these aspects of love, here are a few examples of the way in which the gifts are controlled by the fruits. Goodness is a fruit of the Spirit; it is evident that only a good man can be trusted to make right use of any gift. He who performs deeds of mercy (a *charisma*) should do so with joy (a fruit) (Rom. 12:8). The helmsmen, those who steer the community, the administrators, are entrusted with 'gifts of direction' (*kybernēsis, cf.* cybernetics). They will certainly also require the qualities of patience and kindness if they are to rule according to the example of Christ (1 Cor. 12:28). Faith as a gift, the faith that can move mountains, that can triumph over apparently insuperable obstacles, will degenerate into violence unless controlled by love as gentleness (1 Cor. 13:2). Those who are gifted to lead and preside over the fellowship may often be required to maintain or to make peace. A local church must know whether the utterances of gifted speakers are genuine or phoney, Spirit-inspired, self-induced or demonic. Yet that gift of discernment will cause havoc unless exercised with kindness. To avoid confusion, not to mention boredom, the utterances of prophets and speakers in tongues, of preachers and teachers, should be regulated by the fruits of self-control (1 Cor. 14:32). Illustrations of this relationship between the fruits and the gifts could be multiplied. Character and abilities, virtues and skills, graces and gifts, belong together. The dovetailed gifts of nature and of grace are meant to be controlled and regulated by the love which is joy and peace, patience and kindness, goodness and faithfulness, gentleness and self-control.

The invisible Spirit made visible

In graces and in gifts, the Spirit is manifested, revealed, made visible. For God himself is invisible. 'He lives in the light that no one can approach. No one has ever seen him; no one can ever see him' (1 Tim. 6:16 GNB). Even those who are drawn to Christ do not see God. 'Anyone who hears the Father and learns from him comes to me. This does not mean that anyone has seen the Father; he who is from God is the only one who has seen the Father' (Jn. 6:45-46 GNB). The God 'no one has ever seen', Jesus Christ has made known (Jn. 1:18). But even in Christ, the Word incarnate, God is not seen directly; where he is revealed, he is also hidden. That is also true of the work of the Holy Spirit, God present, God in action. The Spirit is invisible where he is present and unseen where he is active. Like the wind the Spirit cannot be handled or seen. There is something, however, which can be seen, not the wind itself, but its effects. We can see the scudding clouds, the swelling sails, the tossing branches. In this world there are some things we never see and others we see but rarely. No-one has ever seen an electron, the minute particle that revolves around the nucleus of an atom like a planet round the sun. It is seen only indirectly in its effects. If, for example, it is shot through steam it makes an observable impression on the steam, not unlike the tail of a comet. What can be seen is not the electron itself but the impression it makes on that which is visible, the steam. I was brought up on a farm, but it so happens that I have never seen that little, unpopular, subterranean creature, the mole. But I have often seen mole-hills in the pastures, the visible effects produced by creatures I have never seen. The Holy Spirit, God present and in action, can be seen in his effects. His effects are the graces and the gifts.

Christians can be seen. They are living, talking, walking icons of the invisible Lord. In the fruits which the Spirit produces in the character of the Christian the Spirit becomes visible to the world. A loving Christian is visible. A joyful Christian attracts like a magnet. A believer, making peace where there is enmity or acting with patience in trying circumstances, is observed by others. Kindness and goodness are embodied in deeds and faithfulness is apparent in a person's relationships and tasks. He who treats others with gentleness discloses Christ and he who controls himself exhibits the Spirit. The character of a Christian is like an open letter. 'Any man can see it for what it is and read it for himself…a letter that has come from Christ…a letter written not with ink but with the Spirit of the living God, written not on stone tablets but on the pages of the human heart' (2 Cor. 3:2-3 NEB). The invisible Spirit becomes visible in the qualities of character he creates, and a Christlike person is the best demonstration of the Spirit's reality, activity and presence.

The gifts, like the virtues, make the Spirit visible. In the following verse Paul is writing of the *charismata*. 'To each is given the manifestation of the Spirit for the common good' (1 Cor. 12:7). Each Christian is to exhibit the Spirit to the community. 'The Spirit's presence is shown in some way in each person for the good of all' (1 Cor. 12:7 GNB). The Spirit desires to become visible and he becomes visible in the gifts. In the text just quoted the verb ('is given') is in the present continuous tense. The Spirit desires to keep on making himself manifest and he does so in the various abilities, services and forms of work entrusted to believers. The Spirit may become visible in the skill of the artist, the eloquence of the speaker, the wisdom of the ruler. He is manifested in the work of healing, the preaching of the word, the winning of souls. He can be observed in the care of a mother for her children, of a pastor for his flock, of a probation officer for those in need. He is exhibited in the words of the encourager, the gifts of the philanthropist, the initiative of the pioneer, the diligence of the administrator. On the day of Pentecost Peter preached to a crowd the message of Christ crucified, risen and exalted. For the confirmation of his message he drew the attention of the people to the presence and activity of the Holy Spirit, 'which you see and hear' (Acts 2:33). What the crowd could see was the Christians, merry, not with wine, but with the Spirit. What the crowd could hear was the Christians speaking with 'other tongues'. The evidence which confirmed the gospel was fruit (joy) and gift (*glōssolalia*). There was manifestation. The graces and the gifts bear witness. Through both alike the Spirit enables Christians to make Christ known. The two, like husband and wife, should be joined together. For the being of God is his activity; he is what he does and he does what he is. Through what the Christian is and through what he does, through the qualities of character the Spirit produces and through the abilities he imparts, through his graces and through his gifts, the invisible Spirit becomes visible to the world in his effects.

Notes for chapter three

1. John Stott, *Baptism and fullness* (IVP, 1975), p.90.
2. J. S. Stewart, *The Wind of the Spirit* (Hodder and Stoughton, 1968), p.12.
3. John Milton, *Paradise Lost,* Book VII, line 233.
4. Percy Dearmer, from the hymn, 'O Holy Spirit, God, all loveliness is Thine'.
5. John Calvin, *The Institutes of the Christian Religion,* II, iii, 3.
6. William Shakespeare, *The Merchant of Venice*, IV, i, 182.
7. Andrew Reed, from the hymn, 'Spirit divine, attend our prayers'.
8. John Stott, *Baptism and fullness*, p.94.
9. Michael Griffiths, *Cinderella's Betrothal Gifts* (OMF Books, 1978), p.69.

4 Love

The primacy of love

'The fruit of the Spirit is love' (Gal. 5:22). First in the list of the nine fruits of the Spirit, love should also come first in our lives. Let it have absolute priority. Those who are led by the Spirit of God put first things first. Since the purpose of human life is to love and to be loved, love should be priority number one. To be a loving person ought to be a Christian's supreme desire and aim. 'You must want love more than anything else' (1 Cor. 14:1 JB). In that sentence, in the original Greek, Paul employs a verb from the chase, *diōkein*, to pursue. As hounds pursue their quarry, so Christians are urged to go flat-out, to make an eager, strenuous and persistent effort to possess the most excellent gift of love. There are four reasons why love is of first importance: it includes, binds, fulfils and fructifies.

1. *Love includes the other virtues.*   It has already been pointed out, in chapter one, in the section headed 'Not fruits but fruit', that there are not nine separate fruits of the Spirit, of which love is the first. It is not one virtue among others in a list of nine. There is one fruit of the Spirit, the love of God in Jesus Christ our Lord poured into our hearts by the Holy Spirit who has been given to us. The other eight graces in the list are simply aspects of love, ways in which love responds to God and to people, to situations and events, to trials and temptations. We may recall the illustration used. Love is like

a white ray of light; the other virtues are the various colours into which it is broken. So he who has love has all the other virtues: he who is without love has none of them. Love has the primacy not only because it is more important than all the rest but because it includes all the rest.

2. *Love binds everything and everyone together.* It is the principle of coherence in character and in the community. 'And above all these (seven virtues) put on love, which binds everything together in perfect harmony' (Col. 3:14). Picture an oriental putting on his clothes. He finishes dressing by binding all his loose and flowing garments together with a sash or girdle. A Christian is to put on the virtues of Christ, compassion, kindness, humility, gentleness, patience, forbearance, forgiveness. Then 'over all these clothes, to keep them together and complete them', he is to 'put on love' (Col. 3:12-14 JB). Love holds all the other virtues together and completes them. It corrects their distortions, complements their defects, maintains them in due proportion and proper relationship. Through love they cohere. 'Love is the golden chain of all the virtues' (Col. 3:14 J.B.Phillips). That is one possible interpretation of the text. Since, however, in the context, Paul is describing life in the community, he may be referring to the unity of Christians in the one body of Christ. The fellowship includes Jew and Greek, circumcised and uncircumcised, barbarian and Scythian, slave and free. It is love, and love alone, which binds all these diverse elements into one fellowship. It binds, not everything, but everyone, together. Whichever meaning Paul intended, both interpretations are true to fact. Whether of virtues in the character of the individual or of people in the fellowship, it is love which binds them all together in perfect harmony.

3. *Love fulfils the law.* A friendly scribe asked Jesus which of the 613 commandments of the Law of Moses came first in importance. Jesus, in his reply, quoted the first part of the *Shema*, the creed of Israel which Jews recite daily. 'Hear, O Israel: The Lord our God, the Lord is one; and you shall love the Lord your God with all your heart, and with all your soul,

and with all your mind, and with all your strength' (Dt. 6: 4-5; Mk. 12:28-30). The scribe had asked about the first and foremost commandment. Jesus added a second. 'You shall love your neighbour as yourself' (Lv. 19:18). Loving God and loving people go together; they are inseparable. 'There is no other commandment greater than these' (Mk. 12:31). They are the first and the greatest because they include and sum up all the other. 'On these two commandments depend all the law and the prophets' (Mt. 22:40). All that God requires of man, as laid down in the law and the prophets, is derived from and gathered up in these two commandments. 'For the whole law is fulfilled in one word, "You shall love your neighbour as yourself"' (Gal. 5:14; Rom. 13:9). Love is of prime importance because, when we love truly, we are doing all that God requires of us.

4. *Love makes fruitful.* The various *charismata*, the gifts of the Spirit, are effective when exercised in love. Inspired, motivated, permeated and controlled by love, all abilities and aptitudes contribute to the common good. It is not the gifts, but the gifts exercised in love, which build up the community. 'Love builds up' (1 Cor. 8:1). Without love, even the greatest gifts – speaking in tongues, prophecy, insight into mysteries, knowledge, miracle-working faith, almsgiving, martyrdom – are completely worthless (1 Cor. 13:1-3). Whatever gift a person may have it can achieve the purpose for which it was given only if it is used in love. Gifts without love are barren; gifts with love are fruitful. So love has the primacy because without it the noblest gifts cannot be used for the welfare of others, the building up of the community and the glory of God.

God's love for us

To give priority to love, we need to know what it is. We don't know what love is apart from God and his activity in making himself known. 'God is love' (1 Jn. 4:8). That is the ultimate truth about God. Love springs eternally from his Being. It is not one attribute of God among others; love is what God is.

All that God thinks and wills, says and does, arises from and is directed by his love. 'The love that moves the sun and the other stars'[1] never ceases to create, sustain and rule the universe. Because he is love God cannot be discovered by human enquiry or by theological or philosophical speculation. He is known whenever and wherever he makes himself known; and he makes himself known in what he does. 'I am the Lord your God who brought you out of Egypt, where you were slaves' (Ex. 20:2 GNB). In his acts and in his words he makes himself known as love to his redeemed people. 'He taught Moses to know his way and showed the Israelites what he could do. The Lord is compassionate and gracious…as a father has compassion on his children, so has the Lord compassion on all who fear him' (Ps. 103:7-8,13 NEB). This activity of God in making himself known in history is consummated in history, in the life and ministry, in the death and resurrection of Jesus Christ.

We don't find the true meaning of the word *love* by looking it up in any dictionary. It is defined by Jesus Christ. God's love is revealed in his teaching, his deeds and his sacrifice. He taught us to see the Father's love in his providential care for all his creatures and in his indiscriminate kindness to good and bad people alike. There is no limit to his love; he reaches out to men in their need, irrespective of their deserts. He takes the initiative in seeking the lost and freely forgives the sinner who repents. As Jesus taught, so he lived. He put God's love into deeds and made it real. He sought the lost, he befriended the sinner, he restored the fallen, he forgave the penitent. God's love was revealed in signs, in mighty deeds of mercy and compassion. He healed the sick, he liberated the oppressed, he fed the hungry, he consoled the sorrowful. As he lived, so also he died for others. He went to the final limit of self-giving, and in his death on the cross revealed the full extent of God's love. 'God shows his love for us in that while we were yet sinners Christ died for us' (Rom. 5:8). And so it is the life and teaching and the sacrifice and victory of Jesus Christ that define for us the meaning of the word *love*. 'He took this chameleon of a word and gave it a fast colour, so that ever since it is lustred by his teaching and life, and dyed in the crimson of Calvary, and shot through with the sunlight of Easter morning.'[2]

It is this love, as defined by Christ, that Paul describes in chapter 13 of his first letter to the Corinthians. The jewel of love has fifteen facets (1 Cor. 13:4-7). Along with love, two of the other nine fruits of the Spirit, patience and kindness, are included in this character sketch. 'Love is patient and kind.' These two affirmations are followed by eight negatives and one positive. For it is easier to say what love is not than to say what it is. These are, no doubt, eight ways in which some of the Christians at Corinth, like some of us their successors, are unlike Christ. 'Love is not jealous or boastful; it is not arrogant or rude. Love does not insist on its own way; it is not irritable or resentful; it does not rejoice at wrong, but rejoices in the right.' We must do what Paul has done with the eighth negative – give the positive alternative – if these eight are to be facets of the jewel of love. Love rejoices in the gifts and achievements of others. Love is humble, gentle and courteous. Love gives way to others and keeps its cool. It is calm and serene. Love forgives and forgets wrongs and is always glad when right prevails. In conclusion, there are four descriptions of what love does, each including the word *all*. 'Love bears all things, believes all things, hopes all things, endures all things.' Love carries all burdens; it takes God at his word and believes the best about people; it faces the future with unfading hope and triumphant fortitude. It has often been pointed out by commentators that in reading this description, we can substitute the name *Jesus* for the word *love*. Paul, in fact, is painting a portrait of Christ, as we now see him in the gospels. If we are to think rightly about love, and – more important – if we are to walk in love, then we must keep our eyes on this portrait of Jesus Christ. What is love? The answer is, *look at Jesus Christ, and him crucified*.

Our love for God

'We love, because he first loved us' (1 Jn. 4:19). Our love is a response. God's love for us comes before our love for him and for people. His love has priority both in history and in experience. Christ lived, died and rose again before we existed. The Holy Spirit was active within us before ever we became aware of and responded to God's love in Christ. It's because we have been and are loved that we are enabled to love. That is true also in the context of our relationships with one another. If, for example, an infant is deprived of love by his parents; he grows up unable to give love to or receive love from others. Only the loved can love. We look first at our love for God and then at our love for one another.

'You shall love the Lord your God with all your heart, and with all your soul, and with all your might' (Dt. 6:5). This is what God asks of the people he has delivered. The covenant and the law comes after the exodus, the deliverance. Within that relationship of grace love is God's primary and total requirement. His people, with concentrated and undivided allegiance, are to acknowledge him, the unique, the one and only Lord God. The great commandment asks for a total response. 'With all your heart…soul…might' is a poetical way of saying, 'with your whole being'. Every facet of a man's many-sided life, every aspect of his personality, the mind, the will, the emotions, is to be involved and engaged in loving the one and only God. But how? For it is obvious that we cannot love God in precisely the same way that we love human beings. We love those we meet, and the love is mediated through our senses of sight, hearing and touch. But God is invisible, inaudible, intangible, and we cannot meet him directly. What then does it mean to love him? The book in which the great commandment is found, Deuteronomy, brings out the meaning of the verb *to love* by using several other verbs as synonyms. 'And now, Israel, what does the Lord your God require of you, but to fear the Lord your God, to walk in all his ways, to love him, to serve the Lord your God with all your heart and with all your soul, and to keep the commandments and statutes of the Lord, which I command you this day for your good?' (Dt. 10:12-13). To love is to fear, that is, to reverence God; a sentiment which finds expression both in a life of piety and in acts of worship. To love is to walk and to keep; that is to order one's daily conduct in accordance with God's revelation and in obedience to his commandments. To love is to serve; an activity which includes all that is done for God in daily life or offered to him in worship. Emotions and feelings, affections and sentiments, are included, involved and expressed in all these attitudes and activities. Love is devotion and obedience, worship and service. It involves the mind, the affections, the will; it is thought and felt and done. It is a relationship with God, reverent and trustful, warm and loyal, which issues and is expressed in worship and conduct, service and obedience.

In the New Testament we often see people responding with love to the love of God in Christ. Here are four examples, two women, two men. The woman in the house of Simon the Pharisee expressed her love for Jesus profusely. 'She began to wet his feet with her tears, and wiped them with the hair of her head, and kissed his feet, and anointed them with the ointment.' Her love was a response to what Christ had done for her. Forgiven much, she loved much (Lk. 7:36-50). Mary of Bethany, who during the course of his ministry sat at the feet of Jesus listening to his word, at the conclusion of his ministry anointed his feet with costly perfume. She was extravagant. She did not calculate or count the cost. The deep gratitude of her heart was expressed in a lavish gift (Jn. 12:1-8). The apostle Paul, who describes believers as 'those who love God', cannot tolerate the thought that there should be any so-called Christian whose heart is not aflame with love for Jesus. 'If any one has no love for the Lord, let him be accursed' (Rom. 8:28; 1 Cor. 16:22). His own love was a response, personal and passionate, to 'the Son of God, who loved me and gave himself for me' (Gal. 2:20). Constrained by that love, he devoted his life to evangelism, to winning men for Christ. The other great apostle, Peter, who had denied his master three times, was, after the resurrection, questioned three times. 'Simon, son of John, do you love me?' While grieved at the three-fold repetition of the question, Peter protested his love for Jesus. 'Yes, Lord; you know that I love you.' His three affirmations were followed by three charges, 'Feed my lambs....tend my sheep....feed my sheep.' He was entrusted with the pastoral care of Christians (Jn. 21:15-17). In these four selected examples we see love for the Lord Jesus expressed in a variety of ways, in penitence and adoration, in giving and caring, in service and evangelism. As in Deuteronomy Jesus also links love with obedience. 'If you love me, you will keep my commandments ….he who has my commandments and keeps them, he it is who loves me.' This linking of love and obedience is followed by the promise of the Holy Spirit (Jn. 14:15-17, 21). The obedience is the outcome of the love, and the love is the fruit of the Spirit.

It is often said that we can love God *only* by loving people; we can keep the first and great commandment only by keeping the second. The words of the apostle John are often understood in this sense. 'He who does not love his brother whom he has seen, cannot love God whom he has not seen' (1 Jn. 4:20). What John is affirming, however, is that we cannot separate the two loves. We cannot keep the first commandment and not keep the second. But to say that we cannot love God if we don't love people is not to say that loving people is the only way of loving God. Worship is loving God. We love the Lord when we stand in awe of him, when we praise and adore him, when we sing and pray and give thanks. We love him when we do all our work with the intention of pleasing him. The habit of recollection, of turning our thoughts to God habitually during the course of the day, is another way of loving him. We love the Lord whenever we are aware of his presence and do his will. It is also true that we have to deal with him in all our dealings with others. We love the Lord our God when we care for people. The two great commandments are inseparable but they should not be merged or confused.

The four loves

God's love for man, man's love for God, man's love for man — our thinking about these three aspects of love can be confused because, for quite different relationships, we are using one and the same word. For our English word *love* is wide in its range and imprecise in its meaning. It does duty for sentiments of many kinds. For the nature of a sentiment, a complex emotional state, directed towards an object or a person, will depend upon the object or person loved. John loves strawberries and Mary loves painting; Richard loves horses and Joan loves nursing. The word *love* does duty for an appetite and a pastime, for an attachment and an activity. The object of love is more commonly a person, and we may illustrate the many varieties of personal love from the Bible. Abraham loved his only son, Isaac; Jacob fell in love with Rachel; Jonathan loved his friend, David; Nehemiah loved Jerusalem; Mary of Magdala loved Jesus; Paul loved the Christians at Philippi. We use the same verb for parental and romantic love, for friendship and patriotism, for adoration and brotherly love.

The Greeks were more fortunate. In their language there were four main words for love. *Erōs* stands usually for love between the sexes, the love of a man for a woman, and of a woman for a man. The physical and the sexual are involved. Not that a member of the opposite sex was necessarily the object of *erōs;* the word was also used of the desire for truth or beauty, for goodness or for God. *Erōs* is desire, intense and passionate. It is evoked by something or someone of beauty or worth, and by the desire to possess and enjoy the object or person loved. And because *erōs* is the desire to possess for one's own satisfaction or enhancement, it tends to be selfish. 'I want you; you are mine.' *Storgē* belongs to the home. There is a natural and warm affection between the members of a good family. *Storgē* is the love of parents for their children, and of son and daughter for father and mother. It is the love between brothers and sisters, kith and kin. *Philia* is friendship-love. Between friends there is intimacy and understanding. There is an exchange of secrets, a mutual confiding based on trust. While the passionate desire of *erōs* may be absent from *philia*, yet friendship without emotion, affection and tenderness is inconceivable. Here then is love, calm and serene, warm and steadfast. *Agapē* is the love of God, that distinctive love revealed in the character, ministry and death of Jesus Christ. It is God's spontaneous love for man, springing from his own eternal nature. For he does not love us because he sees something of worth in us which he desires for his own fulfilment: it is by loving us that he himself creates our worth and makes us lovable. *Agapē* is the goodwill of God, who in Christ has planned and effected our salvation. It is sacrificial love: Christ giving himself in life and death to the utmost.

While it is certainly a help to clarity of thought, there is also a great danger in distinguishing and defining these four main kinds of love. The first error is to regard the four loves as separate and unrelated. The second error is to exalt *agapē* at the expense of the other three. False contrasts between *agapē* and the other three loves have been made in various ways. There is, it is said, divine love and human love; heavenly and earthly love; the love of redeemed man and the love of natural man; the love which is spontaneous and the love which is caused by something of worth in the one loved; the love which desires to give and the love which desires to get; the love which is sacrificial and the love which is selfish. When these contrasts are made and overdrawn, then the natural loves are demoted and disparaged. As if it were God's intention to deliver us from that which he himself has created, and to transcend our need for sexual love, family affection and human friendship!

God is both our Creator and our Redeemer. It is his purpose that the four loves should interact and be inter-related. *Agapē* is like yeast. When it is put into the dough it gradually transforms it. Grace does not destroy, it fulfils nature. The natural loves, *erōs, storgē* and *philia,* are not replaced or destroyed, they are transformed and fulfilled by *agapē*. The love of one person for another, whether of man and maid, of husband and wife, of parent and child, of friend and friend, can be strengthened, fertilized and enriched by that love which seeks the highest good of the other and gives without counting the cost. Transformed by *agapē*, the loves of desire are sanctified. 'The distinction between selfish love and true love is not identical with the distinction between *erōs* and *agapē*, as if only *agapē* and not also *erōs* could be true love. Could not someone desire another person and yet be able at the same time to give himself? And, on the other hand, is not the person who gives himself also permitted to desire the other? Is there nothing lovable, nothing worth loving, in either lover or beloved?'[3] Even the natural loves are attributed in Scripture to God and to his Son. Hosea likens the love of God for his people to that of a husband for his wife, and to that of a father for his son (Ho. 2:14-20; 11:1-4). 'Jesus in the gospels appears as wholly and utterly human, cuddling children, allowing women to anoint him, aware of the bond of love between himself and Lazarus and his sisters: evidently this love does not exclude *erōs*. Jesus calls his disciples friends.'[4] We should, then, expect the love which is the fruit of the Spirit to influence and penetrate, strengthen and perfect the love between the sexes, the natural affection between kith and kin, the love of friend for friend. God does not work against himself; Creator, Saviour and Sanctifier are one God.

Love and the mind

Let us go back to the first and great commandment. 'You shall love the Lord your God with all your heart, and with all your soul, and with all your mind, and with all your strength.' As we have seen, the various terms are used loosely, as a description of the whole man. Man redeemed, man within the covenant of grace, is to respond to the love of God with the totality of his being. And not only to God, for the first and second commandments are inseparable. In loving people, as in loving God, the whole of a man's personality should be involved. Love mobilizes all the faculties of a man. It includes thinking, doing and feeling; it involves the mind, the will and the emotions. For just as love (*agapē*) includes within itself all the graces, so the phrase *the heart* includes all the other aspects of the inner man. All the energies of the personality, intellectual, volitional, emotional, spring from the heart. As functions of the entire personality, all three aspects – thinking, willing, feeling – are present, in varying degrees, in loving. We shall look at them separately, although in life they are inseparable.

In contemporary speech we tend to contrast the mind and the heart, giving to the former phrase an intellectual and to the latter an emotional connotation. That is not the psychology of the Bible. While in Hebrew thought emotions may be attributed to the heart, it is regarded much more frequently and distinctively as the centre of the intellectual and volitional life of man. The heart thinks, remembers, understands, plans. And so, to love with the heart, is to make full use of our intellectual capacities in caring for others. 'In your minds you must be the same as Christ Jesus' (Phil. 2:5 JB). He made himself nothing, took the form of a servant, suffered death on the cross. That life-style can be reproduced in us by the Spirit, who transforms the mind of the committed Christian (Rom. 12:1-2). The believer's mind-set, his habitual attitude to people, becomes that of the Christ who cared. Every other person is seen as 'the brother for whom Christ died' (1 Cor. 8:11). This new way of seeing people leads the Christian far beyond the circle of his own concerns. 'Let each of you look not only to his own interests, but also to the interests of others' (Phil. 2:4). To do this requires thought and imagination. Jesus gave us the Golden Rule in a positive form. 'So whatever you wish that men would do to you, do so to them; for this is the law and the prophets' (Mt. 7:12). To apply the Golden Rule requires sympathetic imagination. For I must not assume that my neighbour's interests and needs are identical with my own, and then proceed to deal with him on that basis. Instead of projecting my own desires and needs on to him, I must imaginatively put myself in his place, stand in his shoes, see life from his point of view. Narcissus was obsessed with himself. 'The opposite pole to narcissism is objectivity; it is the faculty to see people and things *as they are*, objectively, and to be able to separate this objective picture from a picture which is formed by one's own desires and fears.'[5] Love is that outreaching power of the imagination which enters into the life and seeks the true welfare of the other person. To do this we have to use our heads. Our failure to love truly is often due to our reluctance to think deeply. The quick and easy answer, the simplistic and half-baked solution, can do more harm than good. 'There are many folk today who, with the best intentions in the world, leave a trail of petty ruin behind them because they have nothing more than good intentions. Their philanthrophy, intense only as an emotion, has failed to quicken their brains – to widen their imagination of possibilities and their grasp of realities, to sharpen their intelligence to see what analysis and resynthesis of these would best conduce to the ends of love.'[6] To care for people, especially for those who are out of sight, amid all the complexities of life today, we must use our heads.

Love and the will

In the Old Testament, the word translated *heart* is used more frequently of the will than of the emotions. It is the seat of volition. So to love with the heart is to will the good of the person loved. Love is goodwill and active benevolence. Love is a disposition, a settled will to seek and promote the good and well-being of others. Here the key words are *will* and *action*. Love wills the good of the other person and goes into action to ensure it. That's why love can be commanded. If love were only or mainly an emotion, it would be futile to require it of us. For we can neither produce nor change our inclinations, likings and affections to order. But the Holy Spirit, God at work within us, gives to us the love he requires of us by enabling and ordering our wills. 'For God is at work in you, both *to will* and *to work* for his good pleasure' (Phil. 2:13). Even before his feelings are changed, God makes it possible for a man to will and promote the good of a person he may not like at all, and towards whom he may even feel a strong antipathy. Love is goodwill in action.

The practical nature of love is illustrated in what is perhaps the best known parable of Jesus. A man going down from Jerusalem to Jericho was attacked by robbers who stripped him, beat him up and left him half-dead. A priest and a Levite going down that road saw the man. They may perhaps have thought the unconscious man was dead. Fearing the ceremonial defilement which would have prevented them from performing their duties at the temple, they both walked by on the other side of the road. Then came a member of that mixed and despised race, the schismatic and heretical Samaritans, hated by the Jews. When the Samaritan saw the wounded man he was filled with pity. 'He went over to him, poured oil and wine on his wounds and bandaged them; then he put the man on his own animal and took him to an inn, where he took care of him.' Before leaving next day, the kind Samaritan encouraged the innkeeper to care for the wounded man, gave him money for that purpose, and undertook to reimburse any additional expenditure on his return journey (Lk. 10:30-35 GNB). In this story Jesus portrays love in action. Like the Samaritan, love has legs and arms; it goes to those in need and does things for them. The Samaritan gave from his own resources, bandages, oil, wine, money, time. He acted, dressed the man's wounds, lifted and transported him, took care of him at the inn. The pity which filled his heart was not allowed to evaporate; it moved him to and found expression in action. In his application of the story Jesus underlines those action words, 'You *go*, then, and *do* the same'.

The Holy Spirit is God in action, and the love he pours into our hearts is active love. It goes and does; it expresses and embodies itself in deeds. John had in mind both the teaching and example of Jesus when he wrote, 'My children, our love should not be just words and talk; it must be true love, which shews itself in action' (1 Jn. 3:18 GNB). This practical love the Spirit has produced in the lives of countless numbers of Christians, and many other people of goodwill. Take three great Christians of this 20th century. Albert Schweitzer gave medical treatment to people with malaria, ulcers, dysentery, leprosy and many other sicknesses at Lambarene, West Africa. Kagawa befriended the blind, the beggar, the drunkard, the diseased, in his six-foot-square room in a slum of Kobe, Japan. Mother Teresa cares for the homeless, hungry and sick children in the streets of Calcutta, India. These are well-known and outstanding saints. There is a great multitude of unknown and undistinguished Christians who, like them, have practised the precept, 'Let us put our love...into deeds, and make it real' (1 Jn. 3:18 Moffatt).

Love and emotion

There is an emotional element in love. While the heart in the Bible is regarded primarily and distinctively as the source of thought and will, it is also, as in contemporary usage, the seat of the emotions and affections. To love is to feel. There has been a tendency in the last few decades for some theologians and teachers of ethics to campaign against emotion, and to define love in terms which exclude or devalue it. *Agapē* has been set over against the natural loves. In *erōs*, *storgē* and *philia* there is a strong emotional element. They are characterized by physical, sexual and psychical attraction; they have to do with appetite and desire, inclination and liking. If these natural loves and *agapē* are regarded as mutually exclusive, then the body and the senses, the instincts and the emotions, are taken out of *agapē*. It is spiritualized and dehumanized. 'Vitality, emotion, affectivity are forcibly excluded, leaving a love that is totally unattractive. When love is merely a decision of the will and not also a venture of the heart, it lacks genuine humanity. It lacks depth, warmth, intimacy, tenderness, cordiality.'[7] But the natural loves must not be excluded from *agapē*. They are the material which grace permeates and sanctifies. Taken up, sublimated, transformed, they contribute to *agapē* something of their own energy and warmth. The divine caring, as portrayed by the prophet Hosea, has warmth, emotion, passion, in it. 'How can I give you up, O Ephraim! How can I hand you over, O Israel!.... My heart recoils within me, my compassion grows warm and tender. I will not execute my fierce anger' (Ho. 11:8-9). In the heart of God, as here revealed, there is tension, passion, a tumult of feelings, a conflict between the warm emotions of indignation and compassion. That same heart of God was revealed in Jesus Christ, a man of deep and intense feeling. He wept and grieved; he was elated and rejoiced. He was moved to the depths with warm indignation and compassion. In his consideration and caring there was feeling and emotion, passion and fire.

As it is a mistake to take emotion out of *agapē*, so also it is a mistake to take the liking out of loving. True, they are not the same, but they should not be separated. Since loving has to do primarily with the mind and the will, and liking has to do with attraction, inclination and feeling, it is possible to love people without liking them. It's fortunate that we can and necessary that we should. No man should wait until he feels like it before putting his love into words and deeds. He is under obligation to go and help those in sorrow or need, even if he feels no pity, compassion or concern. Still less must a man confine his caring to those for whom he has a liking. We can love those we dislike and care even for our enemies. Jesus commands this and shows how it is possible by using other action words which draw out the meaning of the verb *to love*. 'Love your enemies, do good to those who hate you, bless those who curse you, pray for those who abuse you' (Lk. 6:27-28). We can love our enemies in what we do for them, say to them and pray for them. If we begin with the third, it may lead on to the other two. 'There is nothing that makes us love a man so much as praying for him; and when you do this sincerely for any man, you have fitted your soul for the performance of anything that is kind and civil towards him.'[8] That was how the Lord Jesus, and his first martyr Stephen, loved their enemies (Lk. 23:34; Acts 7:60). We are, then, under obligation to go and do, to put love into word and action, whether we feel like it or not, whether the other person attracts or repels. That doesn't mean, however, that a Christian ought to stay content with a love which is a matter of the mind and the will only. It should be accepted as a temporary state, something true only of the initial stages of a relationship. Those who *do* love should do it in the hope that eventually they will *feel* love. The psychologist William James taught us to see that, in the long term, and as the result of practice, our feelings tend to catch up with our actions. By regulating our words and actions, which are under the control of mind and will, we can, in due time, evoke the feeling which is not under the direct and immediate control of the will. It is, no doubt, morally admirable to love those we don't like. But who would be thrilled or warmed by the declaration, 'I love you, but I don't like you at all'! By kindling and transforming our emotions, the Holy Spirit can turn our loves into likes.

Four words – power, joy, colour, warmth – may help a little to describe the indescribable, the contribution made by emotion to love. Emotion was the motive, the impelling power, which sent the kind Samaritan into action. He was filled with pity, with feelings of tenderness for the man in distress. He did something because he felt something. Our emotions are a vast reservoir of power. They are the steam in the engine, the petrol in the car. Our instinctive, physical and psychical forces are marshalled for action when feeling is stirred, emotion kindled. The emotions are a source of joy as well as energy. Joy is a derived emotion; it attends our successful strivings and efforts on behalf of a loved person. It is the progressive satisfaction of the desires of love. Joy springs from love and, because they go together, love is often playful and light-hearted; experienced in depth, it is delight, exaltation and ecstasy. Love and joy add a quality to a relationship which may best be likened to colour in nature or in art. There is all the difference in the world between, say, the state opening of Parliament, a Shakespeare play, the Swiss Alps, as seen in black and white and as seen in colour on the television screen. In his famous essay on *Friendship*, Emerson writes, 'The moment we indulge our affections, the earth is metamorphosed.' It changes its form and appearance. We see people not in dull monochrome, but in multicolour and in splendour. One of the biblical symbols of the Holy Spirit is fire, the sign of the presence of God. Fire can destroy or purify; it gives both light and warmth. The Spirit of God not only enlightens the mind and enables the will: he also warms the heart. It is for this warmth of heart that a Christian should aspire.

> O Thou who camest from above,
>   The pure celestial fire to impart,
> Kindle a flame of sacred love
>   On the mean altar of my heart.
>   (C. Wesley)

Philadelphia

The conception of love with warmth in it leads on directly to the study of another term for love. The word *philadelphia*, used five times only in the New Testament, combines the Greek words for love (*philia*) and brother (*adelphos*). It is brotherly love. Attalus II, king of Pergamum, greatly loved his brother Eumenes. So he was called Attalus Philadelphus, and the city he founded, named after him, was Philadelphia (Rev. 3:7). In the year 1682, William Penn founded a city as a haven of refuge for the persecuted. He called his city, the capital of the state of Pennsylvania, Philadelphia. So the word is familiar to us. The reality, for which the name stands, the warm-hearted love and affection between brothers and sisters in the family of God, was characteristic of the early Christians. 'But concerning love of the brethren (*philadelphia*) you have no need to have any one write to you, for you yourselves have been taught by God to love one another.' No need, because they already loved their fellow-Christians at Thessalonica and throughout the whole province of Macedonia. But they were not to be satisfied with the warmth and depth of their love; they were 'to do so more and more' (1 Thes. 4:9-10). For the apostle Peter, *philadelphia* is the climax, the fulfilment of our Christian calling. For our obedient response to the gospel in conversion and baptism is with a view to family love. 'Having purified your souls by your obedience to the truth for a sincere love of the brethren, love one another earnestly from the heart' (1 Pet. 1:22). *Philadelphia* is the goal of the Christian life, personal and corporate. It is the 'noblest jewel in the diadem of early Christianity'.[9]

It was Jesus who taught us that the church is a family. On one occasion the members of his own family came down from Nazareth to Capernaum to see him. 'A crowd was sitting about him; and they said to him, "Your mother and your brothers are outside, asking for you." And he replied, "Who are my mother and my brothers?" And looking around on those who sat about him, he said, "Here are my mother and my brothers! Whoever does the will of God is my brother, and sister, and mother"' (Mk. 3:31-35). All those who listen to God's word, and live in obedience to God's will, are brothers and sisters of Jesus, and so of one another. The small natural family is enlarged to become the family of Jesus, and the love within the small household is transferred to 'the household of God, which is the church of the living God' (1 Tim. 3:15). As brothers and sisters in a family it is fitting that Christians should 'love one another with brotherly affection'. 'Let us have real warm affection for one another as between brothers' (Rom. 12:9-10 J.B. Phillips). As contrasted with *agapē* which is universal in its range, *philadelphia* is the warm and tender affection between brothers and sisters in the family created by Christ. This warm-hearted and intimate love was expressed in 'the sacrament of friendship', the exchange between Christians of the 'holy kiss' of love and peace.

Philadelphia is characteristic of the family or small group. The churches of the apostolic age were house-churches. Assembling in the guest-room of the house of one of their number, the Christians were intimately related, not only vertically to God but also horizontally to one another. If there is to be closeness and intimacy, warmth and affection, the local church must be a small community. If it is large it should be sub-divided into small groups. The worship of the big congregation needs to be supplemented and enriched by the worship of smaller companies. In these a more intimate and affectionate human relationship is possible. Nowadays, having failed to find fellowship in depth in local or parish churches, many Christians have left them. They are meeting in tiny cells, small groups, house-churches. Such groups should be established, and remain *within*, the local church, and contribute to and enrich its fellowship, worship and mission. Within the small company Christians get to know one another in depth and are integrated in the community. Having confidence in one another, they are free to open their hearts in the sharing of experience. Through the study of Scripture they encourage and build one another up, and through prayer co-operate with the purposes of God for people, both within and outside the church.

'Let brotherly love continue.' It is of vital importance that Christians should love one another warmly, and give expression to that love in hospitality and service. Travelling Christians and itinerant ministers are to be entertained in the home, and fellow-believers, arrested and imprisoned for their faith, are to be visited and their sufferings to be alleviated by sympathy and gifts (Heb. 13:1-3). For whether experienced within or manifested outside the church, *philadelphia* is a powerful and effective witness. A family of warm-hearted brothers and sisters is a magnet; it attracts. In the early church, because the love of the little companies of Christians was at a high temperature, men were drawn in from the cold world outside. The church father, Tertullian (AD160-220) records the pagan reaction; 'The heathen are wont to exclaim with wonder, "See how these Christians love one another".' 'It was not as disembodied truth uttered into the air that the Christian "Good News" laid hold of men; it was through the corporate life of the little Christian Societies in the cities of the ancient world. Men coming into contact with such a group felt an atmosphere unlike anything else. Each little group was a centre of attraction which drew men in from the surrounding world.'[10] And it wasn't only a matter of drawing in; there was a going out. For if we nurse the flame of love inside the family of God, its warmth should soon be felt outside. To *philadelphia* we must add *agapē* (2 Pet. 1:7). The love we enjoy as brothers and sisters within the fellowship must issue in that universal love, wide and inclusive, that caring for all people without discrimination which is characteristic of the love of God. 'May the Lord make your love for one another and for all people grow more and more' (1 Thes. 3:12 GNB).

In the upper room on the eve of his crucifixion, Jesus himself drew the attention of his disciples to this relationship between brotherly love and witness. 'A new commandment I give to you, that you love one another; even as I have loved you, that you also love one another.' Why does Jesus call the old commandment – love your neighbour – new? 'Because here it is a question not of loving one's neighbour, but of a special love of Christian to Christian, of *philadelphia* in distinction to universal *agapē*. There is to be a new love-circle, the Christian Church, dependent upon a new love-centre, Christ.'[11] This is to be the badge worn by Christians, the sign by which they will be recognized. 'By this all men will know that you are my disciples, if you have love for one another' (Jn. 13:34-35). 'That is the new commandment, and obedience to it is to be the evidence to the world of true discipleship. If the Church really were like that, if every communicant had for every other a love like that of Christ for him, the power of its witness would be irresistible.'[12]

How love comes and grows

We come now to the crucial question. How does love come to us and increase in us? Love is the fruit of the Spirit; but he does not produce this fruit apart from our co-operation. Those to whom God gives his Holy Spirit… 'have been taught by God to love one another' (1 Thes. 4:8-9). What does the Holy Spirit teach us? How does love come to birth and grow in us? Here is a summary. The first three points refer *primarily* to loving God and the second three to loving people. That, however, is only a matter of emphasis since the two great commandments cannot be separated. All six are ways of loving God, and all six are ways of loving people.

1. *Response* Loving the Lord our God is a response to his initiative in Christ. Love comes to birth when two people meet and there is mutual attraction. Seeing is the stimulus which evokes the love. 'It lies not in our power to love… whoever loved that loved not at first sight.' We may not agree entirely with the poet, Christopher Marlowe. Love is not always evoked at *first* sight, but there is a relationship between seeing and loving. 'And Jesus looking upon him loved him' (Mk. 10:21). It may also be true the other way round; looking upon Jesus we love him. When I was fifteen I read, for the first time, right through the Gospel of Mark. As I did so, something wonderful happened. God revealed his Son to me; with the inner eye, I saw Jesus. That was when I began to love him. We cannot produce love for God by an act of will. It is a Spirit-inspired response to the God who reveals himself to us in Christ. We see and we love.

2. *Indebtedness* The intensity of a person's love for God depends upon the depth of his experience of forgiveness. This is the law of indebtedness. 'Whoever has been forgiven little shows only a little love.' But the one who has been forgiven

81

much, loves much (Lk. 7:43-47 GNB). As a man's awareness of his indebtedness increases, so does his love for the Lord. Love springs from redemption as well as from revelation; from gratitude to the One who loved us and gave himself for us. John Newton served on a slave ship and led a dissipated life in 'misery and wretchedness'. One night, in a terrible storm, he looked death in the face. Next day he was converted through reading the book *The Imitation of Christ*. In a hymn, which has become universally popular, he expresses his sense of indebtedness.

> Amazing grace (how sweet the sound)
>   That saved a wretch like me!
> I once was lost, but now am found,
>   Was blind, but now I see.

Towards the end of his life he wrote, 'My memory is nearly gone, but I remember two things, that I am a great sinner and that Jesus is a great Saviour.' It's seeing these two things together that increases and deepens our love.

3. *Presence* 'All ways of seeking love have one thing in common, namely, putting oneself in the presence of the lovable.'[13] If we are to respond to the Lord who has revealed himself to us and given himself for us, then we must keep on coming into his presence. Love comes to and grows between people who are present to one another. The heart can grow fonder by absence only when absence alternates with presence. Through communion with God, through corporate worship and personal prayer, we grow in loving him. Meditation, disciplined and sustained thought about God; contemplation, looking intently at some picture of God; recollection, the habitual turning of the thoughts to God…these also are ways of putting ourselves into his presence. Of recollection Brother Lawrence writes, 'We must know before we can love. In order to know God, we must often think of him: and when we come to love him, we shall then also think of him often, for our heart will be with our treasure.' Not only in church or in our own quiet room, but as we go about our affairs during the day, we

can grow in the love of God by 'the Practice of the Presence of God'.

4. *Fellowship*   The Lord is present where his disciples are gathered in his name (Mt. 18:20). We can put ourselves into his presence by meeting with them. The fruit of the Spirit, love, is produced and matures, not in the isolated individual, but in the common life of the Body of Christ. The fellowship, created and indwelt by the Holy Spirit, that is the school in which we are taught to love one another. So 'let us consider how to stir up one another to love and good works, not neglecting to meet together' (Heb. 10:24-25). We can meet without loving, but we can't love without meeting. Love arises in the context of our personal relationships with Christians, and it grows as we enter ever more deeply into those relationships. Love comes to maturity in a loving church.

5. *Creation*   It's not only through our fellow-Christians that we can meet, know and love God. The Creator-Spirit is present and operative in creation and we can learn to meet and enjoy God there. Creation is God's; it is not his rival. 'It is not God's will at all to be loved by us *against* the Creation, but rather glorified *through* the Creation, and with the Creation as our starting point.'[14] Through things, through plants and trees, animals and birds, through both the inanimate and the animate creation, and especially through people, we can respond to and love God. That great naturalist and explorer, Edward Wilson of the Antarctic, said, 'Love comes to me by one channel only – the recognition of some beauty, whether mental, moral or physical; colour or sound or form.' According to an ancient collect from the Gelasian Sacramentary, Christians used to pray, 'Pour into our hearts such love toward thee, that we loving thee in all things and above all things, may obtain thy promises which exceed all that we can desire.' It may be symptomatic of our suspicion of nature that, in the 1662 Book of Common Prayer, the phrase *in all things* was left out. We can overcome that negative attitude to creation, and learn to love God above all things, by loving and enjoying God in all the things he has made.

6. *Action* Love grows by action. If we don't use our limbs they atrophy. Deeds keep love alive and well; it becomes strong and sturdy through exercise. The growth of love depends not only on receptivity but also on activity. It is like a tree which grows not only through its roots but also through its leaves and branches. We have already stressed the volitional element in love; it is something to be willed and done. We receive more love as we make use of the love we have in the service of others. As we draw from this well the water rises. Love, whether to God or man, grows by means of the acts which express it. It was the denial of this truth which led a great saint to say, 'What a curious psychology which allows me to kiss my child because I love it, but strictly forbids me to kiss it in order to love it.'[15] By expressing in action the love we have received, we increase and strengthen it.

There is no limit and no end to the love which comes into being and continues to grow in our relationships with God and with one another. Mutual love is the characteristic of life in God's eternal kingdom, where there is no end to its growth, expansion and enrichment. For heaven is not static. There is no end to exploring the boundless ocean of God's love and to meeting, knowing and loving people. The process of being knit together by the love which unites the Father and the Son, the fashioning of the fellowship of the Holy Spirit, goes on through all eternity. Love never ends. In this it differs from the *charismata*. Prophecies and tongues are imperfect and will pass away. Our knowledge in this age is indirect and partial, like the distorted reflections of an object in a bronze mirror. In the age to come it will be superseded by a knowledge which is direct and complete. All the gifts are transitory; the three cardinal graces are permanent. 'So faith, hope, love abide, these three; but the greatest of these is love. Make love your aim' (1 Cor. 13:8-14:1).

Notes for chapter four

1. Dante, *Divine Comedy, Paradiso*, XXXIII, 145.
2. A. C. Craig, *The Sacramental Table* (Harper Bros.), p.50.
3. Hans Küng, *On Being a Christian* (Collins, 1977), p.261.
4. Hans Küng, *ibid*.
5. Erich Fromm, *The Art of Loving* (George Allen and Unwin, 1957), p.118.
6. T. E. Jessop, *Law and Love* (S.C.M., 1940), p.166.
7. Hans Küng, *op. cit.*, p.262.
8. William Law, *A Serious Call* (Everyman Library, 1906), p.294.
9. Herman Gunkel, quoted by A. M. Hunter, *The Interpreter's Bible* (Abingdon Press, 1957), vol. 12, p.104.
10. Elwyn Bevan, *Christianity* (Home University Library, 1932), p.51.
11. G. H. C. Macgregor, *The Gospel of John* (Moffatt New Testament Commentary, Hodder and Stoughton, 1928), pp.283-284.
12. William Temple. *Readings in St. John's Gospel* (Macmillan, 1947), p.223.
13. T. E. Jessop, *op.cit.*, p.135.
14. Gabriel Marcel.
15. F. von Hügel, *Selected Letters* (1927).

5 Joy

Pleasure, happiness and joy

'The fruit of the spirit is...joy.' At the outset, it may be helpful to distinguish joy from pleasure and from happiness, with both of which it is often confused. All three belong together and have much in common; but there are important differences.

'Nature has placed mankind under the governance of two sovereign masters, pain and pleasure.'[1] Like pain, bodily pleasure can be the servant and the friend of man. For while pain may signal the presence of that which is harmful and dangerous to the body, pleasure may signal the presence of that which is beneficial and life-enhancing. Pleasure is the feeling which accompanies the expression of any one instinct; it's a by-product of healthy function and activity. It may spring from the satisfaction of the senses, of hearing and sight, of taste and smell, of touch and movement. The so-called 'higher pleasures', admiring a landscape, reading a book, listening to a symphony, talking to a friend, are of the mind. Sensuous or mental, all pleasures have two severe limitations. They are momentary and fragmentary. They don't last long and they usually give satisfaction to one aspect only of the personality.

Happiness is more lasting than pleasure. It has to do with the personality as a whole. There is a great demand for it! A well-known football magazine includes each week a focus on one particular player. Among the thirty questions put to him is, 'What is your personal ambition?' A large majority of the players questioned give the same answer, to be happy. The desire to be happy is elemental and universal. The common man may never have heard of eudaemonism, but he entirely agrees with those teachers of ethics who maintain the theory that happiness is the highest good. Happiness is not pleasure, nor is it the sum total of all the pleasures. When, for example, we speak of a happy marriage, we have in mind something more than the pleasures, whether of body or mind, within that relationship. The key words here are duration, harmony and wholeness. Happiness is more pervasive and stable than pleasure; if less intense, it continues for some time. It's like harmony in music. A person is happy, not when there is conflict within, but when all his instinctive emotions, inclinations and powers co-operate and find harmonious expression. His personality *as a whole* finds satisfaction and fulfilment in his activities and relationships.

Happiness, like pleasure, however, has its limitations. In spite of the popular expectation, no-one can be happy all the time. It's in fairy stories, not in real life, that people live 'happily ever afterwards'. Those who expect to be happy all the time should reflect on the Arab proverb, 'All sunshine makes a desert.' The derivation of the word *happiness* from the archaic *hap*, chance, luck, fortune, provides a clue. Happiness depends upon good fortune, on favourable circumstances. It departs with them. A boy with a raging toothache, a workman who has been made redundant, a mother whose daughter has been killed in a car accident, cannot at that time be happy. Joy, unlike happiness, does not depend on favourable circumstances. The fortunes of Paul and Silas in the gaol at Philippi were at a low ebb. With backs bruised and bleeding from a severe beating they were in a dark and stuffy inner prison, their feet fixed in the stocks. Yet, at midnight, they were singing praises to God. They were filled with joy (Acts 16:25).

We shall describe the following six characteristics of joy in this chapter:

1. The source of all joy is God – it springs from his love and his activity.

2. This joy of God is revealed and embodied in Jesus

Christ; we receive it through our response to and relationship with him.

3. Joy springs from love; wherever there is love, there is joy.

4. Joy is the by-product of creative activity and achievement.

5. Joy is expressed primarily in worship.

6. Joy is only partially present in this life; it is complete in heaven.

The joy of God

God is love, and the joy of God springs eternally from what he is, that is, from his love. In overflowing love he gives himself in the activities of creating and re-creating, of making and making whole. God is both creator and redeemer; it is from the two-fold activity of God in creation and redemption that his joy overflows. When he created the world, 'the morning stars sang together, and all the sons of God shouted for joy' (Jb. 38:7). God never ceases to create. He visits the earth, sends the rain, causes the plants to grow, fills the valleys with wheat and the pastures with flocks. In response to his creative activity, 'everything shouts and sings for joy' (Ps. 65:9-13 GNB). Joy attends his redemptive as well as his creative activity. Saved from Babylonian captivity and exile, 'the ransomed of the Lord shall return, and come to Zion with singing; everlasting joy shall be upon their heads; they shall obtain joy and gladness, and sorrow and sighing shall flee away' (Is. 35:10). The salvation of the individual, like that of the people of God, is celebrated with joy. The shepherd rejoices over the sheep which was lost and is found. He calls his neighbours together to a celebration feast, saying, 'Rejoice with me, for I have found my sheep which was lost' (Lk. 15:6). 'Such is the character of God; it is his good pleasure that the lost should be redeemed because they are his; their wanderings have caused him pain, and he rejoices over their return home. It is the redemptive joy of God of which Jesus speaks, the joy in forgiving.'[2]

God creates through his Word. The Word became flesh and dwelt among us, and gave up himself for us in order to re-create us. It is in terms of joy that Jesus describes his ministry and mission. A Jewish wedding was a time of gladness, joy and festivity. Jesus likens himself to the bridegroom and his disciples to the chief guests. His coming brings in the time of joy, during which sadness, gloom and fasting are not appropriate (Mt. 9:15). The kingdom of God which he preached, and the nature of which he disclosed in his parables, is joy, great and glorious. 'The kingdom of heaven is like treasure hidden in a field, which a man found and covered up; then *in his joy* he goes and sells all that he has and buys that field' (Mt. 13:44). 'When that great joy, surpassing all measure, seizes a man, it carries him away, penetrates his inmost being, subjugates his mind. All else seems valueless compared with that surpassing worth. No price is too great to pay.'[3] The kingdom is God reigning in power and love, his utterly gracious yet utterly demanding sovereignty over us and over the world. That kingdom is present in the person and mission of Jesus. To be found by and to find God in Christ, to know and to love him, to trust and to obey him, that is man's supreme joy.

In his discourses in the upper room, Jesus speaks of 'my joy', that is his own characteristic and unique joy. This he promises to share with his disciples. 'These things I have spoken to you, that my joy may be in you, and that your joy may be full' (Jn. 15:11). 'The promise and hope is not only that we may be joyful as our Master is joyful – my joy – but that joy of the same substance and quality as his – the joy which is mine – may be in us.'[4] The distinctive joy of Jesus springs from his perfect communion with the Father and from his redemptive activity for men. The source of both is love. The Father loves the Son and the Son loves the Father. From that perfect and reciprocal love, joy springs eternally. The filial virtues of Jesus, reverence, obedience and trust, are components of love. Jesus loves God completely, and from his heart filled with love his joy overflows. Jesus also loves us completely, and in love he gave himself up for us. He endured the cross for 'the joy that was set before him' – 'the joy of a world by him redeemed from selfishness and mutual destruction to love and abundant life.'[5]

Jesus our joy

The promise made by Jesus on the night of his betrayal, to share his own joy with the disciples, was fulfilled after his resurrection. Joy became the outstanding characteristic of Christian life in the apostolic age. It was not, like happiness, dependent on favourable circumstances; it was constant. 'Rejoice in the Lord always; again I will say, Rejoice' (Phil. 4:4). This perpetual joy is 'in the Lord', in Jesus crucified, risen and reigning. It springs from the redemption won by him, from his resurrection from the dead and from his presence within the hearts of believers through the Holy Spirit.

Joy comes from Christ crucified, from his finished work on the cross, from the completed activity of redemption. It is the joy of the redeemed, the gladness of those who receive and rest upon the deliverance won by Christ. Joy comes from hearing and believing the gospel (Acts 16:31,34). It is the joy of forgiveness and of restored fellowship with God (Rom. 4:7; 5:1-2). Those who believe in the Saviour are filled by the Holy Spirit with all joy and peace (Rom. 15:13). When the pilgrim, Christian, came to the cross, his burden of sin and guilt was 'loosed from off his shoulders and fell from off his back...*then* was Christian glad and lightsome, and said with a merry heart, "He hath given me rest by his sorrow, and life by his death".'⁶

Before his death Jesus had spoken of the great and abiding joy that would fill the hearts of his disciples after his resurrection. 'When a woman is in travail she has sorrow, because her hour has come; but when she is delivered of the child, she no longer remembers the anguish, for joy that a child is born into the world. So you have sorrow now, but I will see you again and your hearts will rejoice, and no one will take your joy from you' (Jn. 16:21-22). This promise was fulfilled at Easter. 'Then the disciples were glad when they saw the Lord' (Jn. 20:20). It is of this abiding and immense joy in the risen Lord, present though invisible, that Peter writes to second generation Christians. 'Blessed be the God and Father of our Lord Jesus Christ! By his great mercy we have been born anew to a living hope through the resurrection of Jesus

Christ from the dead…Without having seen him you love him; though you do not now see him you believe in him and rejoice with unutterable and exalted joy' (1 Pet. 1:3,8). The relationship between love and joy and between believing and rejoicing, is here made explicit. Jesus, raised from the dead, alive for evermore, is the 'joy of loving hearts'.

The risen Lord is *present* with his disciples to the close of the age (Mt. 28:20). He makes his home in the hearts of believers through the Holy Spirit. Joy springs from his presence within. 'I stand at the door and knock; if anyone hears my voice and opens the door, I will come into his house' (Rev. 3:20 GNB). Joy takes possession of the heart which receives Christ as guest, and so, as a chorus puts it:

> If you want joy, real joy, wonderful joy,
>   Let Jesus come into your heart.

Joy and love

As already observed, many people believe that happiness is the chief end of life, and they have made it their ambition to attain it. They are usually disappointed and frustrated. For happiness is shy and elusive, and those who seek it directly rarely find it. Real happiness, deep and abiding, that is, joy, is a by-product of love. Go after it and it evades and escapes you. Live for others and it comes to you unsought and unawares. The Greek word for this second of the fruits of the Spirit, *chara*, points to this relationship between joy and love. '*Charis* and *chara*, grace and joy, grew from the same Greek root. The joy that was the fruit of the Spirit sprang from a life that was gracious and kind, full of goodwill, generous to impart itself to others, glad when they accepted and rejoiced with it, but forgiving and still singing, when men rejected and persecuted it.'[7]

The joy of Jesus was the fruit of his love for people. When he likened himself to the bridegroom and his disciples to the guests at a wedding, he was sitting at dinner with tax-collectors and outcasts. Jesus enjoyed feasts and social life. He liked being with people. Because he lived for others all the time he was joyful at all times, for his joy could co-exist with sorrow. His joy was in people as well as in God. In his allegory of the vine he puts love and joy together. 'These things I have spoken to you, that my joy may be in you, and that your joy may be full. This is my commandment, that you love one another as I have loved you' (Jn. 15:11-12). It is as the disciples love one another as Jesus loves them that they will experience to the full the distinctive joy of Jesus, the joy which springs from the reciprocal love of the Father and the Son. Where there is love, there is joy.

Joy is people, the people you love. That's how Paul, missionary and pastor, describes his converts. 'For what is our hope or joy or crown of boasting before our Lord Jesus at his coming? Is it not you? For you are our glory and joy' (1 Thes. 2:19-20). Our joy – you! The *you* may be singular or plural, the individual or the fellowship. Paul writes to Philemon, 'For I have derived much joy and comfort from your love, my brother' (Phm. 7). Because the church at Philippi had shown concern for him, a prisoner, by sending to him a gift of money, he responded by writing the 'Epistle of Joy'. 'Rejoice, you no less than I, and let us share our joy' (Phil. 2:18 NEB). Knit together in love, Christians experience the joy of the Lord as they help and serve one another. Like love, joy is not confined to the Christian fellowship. In romantic love and marriage, between the members of a family, among friends, in all affectionate and caring relationships, there is joy. It springs from all four kinds of love, from *erōs* and *storgē*, from *philia* and *agapē*. Of the Lady Greensleeves, her lover writes – 'Greensleeves was all my joy, Greensleeves was my delight.'[8] Affection within the family is a source of lasting happiness. Here is the testimony of a young mother. 'I was scurrying round the kitchen getting breakfast for my husband and our three children. The sun was streaming in, the sound of frying bacon mingled with the casual chatter of husband and children. As I looked at them I was so overwhelmed by their beauty that tears sprung to my eyes, and I was all joy.'[9] In his treatise *Christian Friendship*, Ailred, abbot of Rievaulx (1109-67), writes of the relationship between pleasure, happiness and joy, on the one hand, and friendship, affection and love, on the other. 'Nothing seemed more attractive to me, nothing more pleasurable or more worth-while than to be loved and to love. The happiest man is he who finds perfect rest in the affections of those around him.' Whenever romantic love, family affection and friendship are permeated and strengthened by *agapē*, by caring, by self-giving love, there is joy. 'The fruit of the Spirit is love, joy'…and the joy comes from the love.

Joy and activity

We have seen in the Bible that the joy of God springs from his creative activity. It is not otherwise with human joy. Made in the image of God, man can respond to and share in the creative activity of God. To the degree in which he does this, he experiences joy. It is the by-product of any activity which takes a man out of himself. For it is when we are preoccupied with our work that joy comes to us unawares. The task may be cooking or making clothes, gardening or carpentry, speaking or writing, painting or designing, engineering or building. A child building a sand-castle on the beach, a boy making a model aeroplane, are surprised by joy. The farmer and the fisherman, the teacher and the doctor, delivered from self-concern because preoccupied with their tasks, find joy in their work. Joy accompanies the successful performance of any task. 'It is God's joy which is with the scientist as he pursues his researches, with the artist in the exercise of his craft, with the administrator as he brings order out of muddle, with parents as they nurture their children, with friends as they gossip and children as they play together.'[10] Those who find joy in their daily work are singularly fortunate. 'Blessed is he who has found his work; let him ask no other blessedness.'[11] Not all of us can find that blessedness. In our industrial society, with its mass production, the jobs of many people are dull and monotonous, repetitive and unsatisfying. The joy a man cannot find in his job, he may find in his second job, the hobby or activity, skill or service in which he engages during his leisure time.

This is especially true of voluntary service, the unpaid

work we do for people and for the Lord. Henry Drummond, author and evangelist, who interpreted the Christian life in terms of the continuity to be seen in the natural order, saw joy as the *inevitable* outcome of service. 'I defy any man to do something for somebody, comfort them, help them, and not come back happier and full of joy. This is cause and effect and anyone can get joy in this way.' As with God, so with man; joy springs from self-giving. Whether it is in the giving of money or of time, of help or of service, we soon learn from experience the truth of the words of Jesus, 'Happiness lies more in giving than in receiving' (Acts 20:35 NEB). A contemporary interpreter of human conduct, the psychologist Abraham Maslow, draws attention to the same law. 'I never met a happy individual who was not committed to a job or cause outside himself. Because such people have a mission in life, they are not self-centred and introspective. For them happiness is the by-product of work and duty.'[12]

Joy and worship

Joy, like love, grows by means of the acts which express it. There are, according to the Bible, appropriate occasions for the expression of joy. Among those mentioned are: the birth and the weaning of a child, marriage, harvest-home, the return of a lost son, finding treasure, recovery from sickness, deliverance from danger, victory in battle. Such events were celebrated with feasting, dancing, music, singing. It is significant, however, that in the Old Testament the various Hebrew words translated as *joy* and *rejoicing* are used most often of the cult, the organized system of worship. The great festivals of Israel were in fact just that, festivals. They were celebrated with joy and gladness. When sacrifice was offered at the Temple, 'the sons of Aaron shouted, they sounded the trumpets, they made a great noise, and the singers praised him with their voices in sweet and full-toned melody' (Ecclus. 50:16, 18). The Hebrews gave expression to their joy vocally (speaking, singing, shouting), musically (through stringed, wind and percussion instruments) and physically (dancing, leaping, lifting hands, clapping, kneeling, prostration).

Joy was also characteristic of Christian worship. The first disciples 'broke bread together in their homes, sharing meals with simple joy' (Acts 2:46 J. B. Phillips). Under the inspiration of the Holy Spirit the Christians assembled were free to contribute to and participate actively in the common worship. Paul exhorts them to 'be filled with the Spirit, addressing one another in psalms and hymns and spiritual songs, singing and making melody to the Lord with all your heart' (Eph. 5:18-19). The celebration of Christ, of his incarnation, sacrifice, resurrection and presence, should be the supremely happy occasion. Is this a reason, perhaps *the* reason, for the rapid growth and widespread appeal of the pentecostal and charismatic movements? Like a magnet, joy draws; a happy assembly attracts. 'Joy is, in fact, a mark of the usual pentecostal assembly. Most of those in attendance at the meeting seem glad to be there. The Pentecostal often asks why joy and its expression should be permitted to almost every kind of human convocation except the Church. Pentecostals argue that it is an elementary human desire to wish to be happy and a fundamental responsibility of the church to provide opportunity and expression for this happiness.'[13]

When Christians are not assembled for worship, but dispersed in the world, joy will continue to find expression in praise and thanksgiving. For the spontaneous praise of the heart cannot be confined to the periods of congregational worship. 'Through Jesus, then, let us continually offer up to God the sacrifice of praise' (Heb. 13:15 NEB). Happiness, as we have seen, depends on favourable circumstances; joy does not. If our attitude to and relationship with the Lord is right, we can be joyful at all times and grateful in all circumstances. 'Be always joyful; pray continually; give thanks whatever happens; for this is what God in Christ wills for you' (1 Thes. 5:16-18 NEB). While this is easier said than done, the habit, once established, is the open secret of joy or abiding happiness. 'If anyone would tell you the shortest, surest way to all happiness, and all perfection, he must tell you to make a rule to yourself to thank and praise God for everything that happens to you.'[14] Some Christians today have re-discovered this ancient secret of praising and thanking God in all life's incidents and happenings. They have learned to strengthen and increase the joy they already have, by expressing it. Praising and thanking God, at all times and in all places, through Jesus Christ, Saviour and Mediator, they are filled with joy by the Holy Spirit.

Man's chief end

At the beginning of this chapter attention was drawn to the ambition of the ordinary man, to be happy. It's a sound ambition if happiness is interpreted as blessedness, as joy. For joy is the chief end of man, the supreme purpose for which he is created and re-created. God intends that joy for man, here and now, in this life. The promise of Jesus to share his own distinctive joy with his disciples was fulfilled when he was raised from the dead. In this present life Christians have immense joy in the risen Lord. 'Though you do not now see him you rejoice with unutterable and exalted joy' (1 Pet. 1:8). The apostles preached, wrote and laboured that others might share that joy here and now. 'We write this in order that the joy of us all may be complete' (1 Jn. 1:4 NEB). 'We work with you for your joy' (2 Cor. 1:24). This is the meaning and the objective of the Christian life. 'Man is to give glory to the true God and rejoice in God's and his own existence, for this by itself is meaningful enough. Joy is the meaning of human life, joy in thanksgiving and thanksgiving as joy.' [15]

This joy, which the believer is given in the present, is an anticipation of the joy of heaven. The Spirit gives us joy, real joy, wonderful joy, now; but the joy he gives is partial not complete. He is the *arrabōn*, the pledge, the guarantee, of our heavenly inheritance until we come into full possession of it (Eph. 1:14). The first instalment is not the full sum; the *hors d'oeuvre* is not the whole meal. The Spirit is the foretaste of the heavenly feast. It is not God's will that we should find complete and final satisfaction in the pleasures and joys of this present age. 'Our Father refreshes us on the journey with some pleasant inns, but will not encourage us to mistake them for home.' [16] And so the Spirit gives joy with hope, with the desire and expectation of greater joy to come. 'We rejoice in our hope of sharing the glory of God' (Rom. 5:2).

Joy in heaven is the fulfilment of the joy we already have here on earth. It will no longer be intertwined with sorrow, for in the final state the desires of love are no longer frustrated and denied but satisfied and fulfilled. In heaven joy finds expression in spontaneous, unanimous and unceasing worship. There, rest and creative activity belong together, and the reward for faithful service on earth is a larger sphere of service. Heaven is the communion of saints; we shall all be knit together in love. In the one fellowship of the Holy Spirit, through Jesus Christ who loves us, we shall all know, see and love God. From his love for us, and our love for him and for one another, joy springs eternal. 'Thou dost show me the path of life; in thy presence there is fulness of joy, in thy right hand are pleasures for evermore' (Ps.16:11). 'What is the chief end of man?... to glorify God and to enjoy him for ever.'[17]

Notes for chapter five

1. Jeremy Bentham, *Principles of Morals and Legislation.*
2. J. Jeremias, *The Parables of Jesus* (S.C.M., 1954), pp.107-108.
3. *Ibid.*, p.140.
4. William Temple, *Readings in St. John's Gospel* (Macmillan, 1947), p.265.
5. *Ibid.*, p.265.
6. John Bunyan, *The Pilgrim's Progress.*
7. R. T. Stamm, *The Interpreter's Bible* (Nelson, 1953), vol. 10, p.566.
8. Anon. From *A Handful of Pleasant Delites* (1584).
9. J. E. Lagemann, *Reader's Digest*, November 1967.
10. H. A. Williams, *The Joy of God* (Mitchell Beazley, 1979), p.56.
11. Thomas Carlyle, *Past and Present*, chap. II.
12. Quoted by J. E. Lagemann, *Reader's Digest*, November 1967.
13. F. D. Bruner, *A Theology of the Holy Spirit* (Hodder and Stoughton, 1971), pp.133-134.
14. William Law, *A Serious Call* (Everyman Library, 1906), p.197.
15. J. Moltmann, *Theology and Joy* (S.C.M., 1971), p.42.
16. C.S. Lewis, *The Problem of Pain* (Geoffrey Bles, 1940), p.103
17. The Shorter Catechism.

6 Peace

Shalōm

'The fruit of the Spirit is…peace.' We use that word nowadays with a reduced and limited meaning. Its connotation is
largely negative. Peace is the cessation or the absence of
strife. In the political, international and military spheres
peace is the state of affairs following the ceasing of hostilities.
If there is no war, we are at peace. As individuals, we also
tend to use the word in this same negative and diminished
way. A harassed father, when asked by his three boisterous
children what present he would like for Christmas, replied, 'a
little peace'. The current phrase 'peace and quiet' points in
the same direction. Peace is the absence of noise and
disturbance. It is enjoyed when we are 'far from the madding
crowd's ignoble strife'.

We turn from this limited and negative, to the full and
positive meaning of the word *peace* as it is found in Scripture.
Our English word *peace* translates the Greek word *eirēnē*. In
the Greek version of the Old Testament, the Septuagint,
eirēnē is used to translate the Hebrew word *shalōm*. The root
meaning of *shalōm* is wholeness. It describes the state of
integrity, harmony and completeness, of a person in
community, and of a community of persons in right relationship with one another and with God. A person has peace
when he has the good life in its fulness. It includes good
health, refreshing sleep, soundness of body and mind,
material prosperity, safety and security, a long life and a
tranquil death. This welfare of the individual is bound up

inseparably with that of the family and the community. There is domestic and communal peace when there is wealth, fertility, prosperity and security. It is a state of plenty in which the earth and the animals are fertile and there is an abundance of food and wealth. It is a state of security, domestic, social and political; of freedom from fear and deliverance from enemies. In this last sense it may also refer to the absence or the ending of war, or to the making of a treaty.

The prosperity and the security are based on right personal relationships, the relationships of the people to one another and to God. *Shalōm* is 'the harmony of a caring community, informed at every point by its awareness of God'.[1] The harmonious and caring relationships of the people are based upon right relationships with God. This complex of relationships created and renewed by God is 'the covenant of peace' (Ezk. 37:26).

Shalōm is described in a superb poem. 'But once more (on return from exile) God will send us his spirit. The waste land will become fertile, and fields will produce rich crops. Everywhere in the land righteousness and justice will be done. Because everyone will do what is right, there will be peace and security for ever. God's people will be free from worries, and their homes peaceful and safe' (Is. 32:15-18 GNB). Fertility, prosperity, safety and security are the effect, the outcome, the fruit of righteousness. When men are in right relationship with one another and with God, there is lasting prosperity, security and peace, and a fulfilment of the goals of human life. This new order is created when 'the Spirit is poured upon us from on high' (Is. 32:15). *Shalōm* is the fruit of the Spirit.

The peace of Christ

In the gospels we must give the word *peace* that full and positive content that the word *shalōm* has in the Old Testament. The Spirit, the source of peace, anointed Jesus at his baptism, and, resting upon him, enabled him for his ministry, powerful in word and deed. He went forth with the message of peace, *i.e.* of wholeness, of salvation. 'You know the word which he (God) sent to Israel, preaching good news of peace by Jesus Christ' (Acts 10:36). This mission of peace was extended widely through the twelve apostles and the seventy disciples. Those preachers of the gospel were to offer to others the *shalōm*, the salvation, which Jesus was bringing. 'Peace be to this house!' This power-laden word of greeting was regarded as objective: the salutation conveyed what it announced. It would rest upon and bear fruit in 'a son of peace', one who accepted the message of salvation. If rejected, 'the peace' returned to the giver (Lk. 10:5-6).

Jesus knew that the offer of salvation would be accepted by some and rejected by others. Therefore, his message would result in division as well as in reconciliation. 'Do not think that I have come to bring peace on earth; I have not come to bring peace, but a sword' (Mt. 10:34). He was no false prophet 'saying, "Peace, peace," when there is no peace' (Je. 6:14). He was the bearer of the true peace which is the effect of righteousness; not of the false and easy peace which has to do with moral compromise and the surrender of principle. In this sinful world, the message and mission of Jesus would be like a sword. Since some would accept and some reject the message, the inevitable result would be division in the family and in society. Yet that was, and is, the inevitable result, not the primary purpose of his mission. Jesus came with the good news of peace, and his deeds, like his words, had to do with the establishment of *shalōm*. For when he healed the bodies or the minds of men, he was removing disorder and restoring wholeness. The miracles were signs of salvation, of the fulness of life which God was giving to men in Christ. Those who had been healed, made whole, were dismissed with the words, 'go in peace'.

The peace which Christ proclaimed, he himself possessed. Since he refers to it as 'my peace', it must be regarded as a distinctive quality of his own character and personality. Jesus, when he left this world, had no material bequests to make to his relatives and disciples. At the end his only material possessions, the clothes he wore, were taken by the four soldiers who had crucified·him. But he had a spiritual legacy for his disciples. 'Peace I leave with you; my peace I

101

give to you' (Jn. 14:27). This peace has three characteristics.

1. *The peace of Christ is an inward peace, not dependent on outward circumstances.* Had his peace depended on favourable circumstances he would soon have lost it. His popularity at the beginning of his ministry in Galilee soon began to wane. Many of his friends and disciples fell away, and the hostility of the Pharisees and the Sadducees steadily increased. When he set his face to go to Jerusalem, the shadows deepened, the storm clouds gathered. It was when the circumstances were most adverse and threatening, in the upper room on the eve of his crucifixion, that Jesus spoke of his peace. 'My peace I give you; not as the world gives do I give to you.' The world cannot give the peace which is independent of outward circumstances. That kind of peace is the legacy of Christ, who offers it as the alternative to fear and consternation. 'Let not your hearts be troubled, neither let them be afraid' (Jn. 14:27).

2. *The peace of Christ is related to his vocation.* A single purpose ran through, dominated and integrated his life. Reference has already been made in chapter two to the single-mindedness and whole-heartedness with which Jesus devoted himself to his vocation. His ministry is like a river. It flows in one direction and is resistless in its flow. Restlessness, especially in the young, is often due to a lack of direction and aim. Man needs a purpose into which, like tributaries into a river, all the diverse interests and energies of his life can flow. Jesus had a purpose from which he could not be deflected and to which he was utterly loyal. So he possessed and he gives 'that peace which flows serene and deep, a river in the soul'.[2]

3. *The peace of Christ springs from his obedience.* He willed to do God's will. In the obedience of Jesus to the will of God we have the open secret of his peace. 'I am in the Father and the Father in me...I do as the Father has commanded me' (Jn. 14:11, 31). Jesus lived in perfect union with the Father, a union of thought, heart and will. Isaiah in Babylon, addressing the Jewish exiles, links obedience and *shalōm*. 'O that you had hearkened to my commandments! Then your peace would

have been like a river' (Is. 48:18). The prophet has in mind the difference between a wadi, the water of which disappears in time of drought, and a river like the ever-flowing Euphrates. To live in obedience to the will of God is to have a living, flowing, perennial peace. The peace which comes of willing one thing, and that one thing the will of God, is Christ's legacy to us.

Peace with God

The legacy of Christ, his peace, is mediated to believers through his death and resurrection. Promised on the eve of his death, it is the gift of the risen Lord to his disciples. The old greeting has a new content. 'Jesus came and stood among them and said to them, "Peace be with you." When he had said this, he showed them his hands and his side' (Jn. 20:19-20). The wounds, the proof of his identity, also disclose the quality of his Body – it's the Body of one 'having been crucified'. The sacrifice of the cross with its continuing efficacy, is included in the renewed and larger life of the living Lord. It is the risen Lord who was crucified, who imparts peace, *shalom*, salvation, the sum total of spiritual benefits and blessings. Through Christ crucified and risen we have peace with God.

If two people, formerly friends, have quarrelled and are living in a state of enmity, they can enjoy peace only if they are reconciled. The apostle Paul uses this metaphor of reconciliation to interpret what Christ has done for us. Our human condition was that of alienation from God. There was an estrangement between us and God, a state of hostility. Before Christ came to the rescue we 'were far off…separated …alienated…strangers…without God in the world' (Eph. 2:12-13). That great gulf between men and God, Christ came to bridge. 'While we were enemies we were reconciled to God' (Rom. 5:10). We were reconciled to God by God. For it was God himself who took the initiative and was active throughout the whole course of Christ's ministry, consummated in his atoning death on the cross. 'God was in Christ, reconciling the world unto himself' (2 Cor. 5:19 AV). This activity of God in Christ is complete, 'We have now received our reconciliation' and has created an entirely new situation and status for man. 'We were God's enemies, but he made us his friends through the death of his Son…Because of our sins he was handed over to die, and he was raised to life in order to put us right with God. Now that we have been put right with God through faith, *we have peace with God* through our Lord Jesus Christ' (Rom. 5:10; 4:25; 5:1 GNB).

Peace is a gift. It's not a human but a divine achievement. God has made it. He has made us his friends, he has reconciled us by the death of his Son. Peace, *shalōm*, the sum total of Christ's benefits and blessings, becomes ours through faith; it is a gift received through surrender to Christ. Peace is a fruit of the Spirit, produced in those who are reconciled to God by the death of his Son, and are saved by his life (Rom. 5:10). Both the death and the life, the cross and the resurrection, are involved. The experience of Pilgrim in Bunyan's allegory may be referred to again. For not only did he receive joy, he also received peace at the cross and the sepulchre. 'Then was Christian glad and lightsome, and said, with a merry heart, "He hath given me *rest* by his sorrow, and life by his death." Now as he stood looking and weeping, behold three shining ones came to him and saluted him with "*Peace* be to thee".' Then he received the forgiveness of God, was clothed with the righteousness of Christ and the Holy Spirit put his mark of ownership upon him. He was at peace with God through Christ crucified and risen.

Peace within

From the peace with God comes the peace of God. The subjective peace of fellowship with God through Christ springs from the objective peace of reconciliation with God through Christ. Peace is both reconciliation and tranquillity. Restored to harmony with God, we experience harmony within. This inner serenity is not only received, it is also maintained, by faith. 'Thou dost keep him in perfect peace, whose mind is stayed on thee, because he trusts in thee. Trust in the Lord for ever, for the Lord God is an everlasting rock' (Is. 26:3-4). Men of constant mind are kept in peace because they trust in the eternally stable and reliable God. That is the implication of the blessing, 'May the God of hope fill you with all joy and peace in believing' (Rom. 15:13). It's the believing heart that is brim-full of joy and peace.

Paul likens this peace of God to a sentry. 'The peace of God, which is of far more worth than human reasoning, will keep guard over your hearts and your thoughts, in Christ Jesus' (Phil. 4:7 NEB margin). The peace from God can preserve and keep the heart of man in tranquillity. That is the testimony of the Indian Christian mystic Sadhu Sundar Singh. Early one morning (it was 4.30 a.m.) in his bedroom, he was in despair. He had resolved to commit suicide when he had a vision of Christ. 'So I fell at his feet and got this wonderful Peace which I could not get anywhere else. When I got up the vision had all but disappeared; but although the vision disappeared the Peace and Joy have *remained* with me ever since.'[3] The believer guarded by God's peace, however, must himself keep guard if he is to retain inner peace. Paul's words 'we have peace with God' can also be translated, 'let us have peace with God'. Translated in that way, they are an exhortation, something required of us. The gift is also a task. Indeed, it would be contrary to the testimony of most of the saints to claim that a Christian can be kept in peace without difficulty. The guard is threatened by enemies within and without.

John Bunyan's allegory, *Pilgrim's Progress*, is true to the experience of most believers. As we have seen, Christian finds peace at the cross, where he loses his burden. But he still has to face 'many a conflict, many a doubt, fighting and fears within, without', before he reaches the celestial city. Those conflicts don't all come, as Charlotte Elliott's hymn suggests, before we come to the Lamb of God, who takes away the sin of the world. The inner conflict described by Paul in Romans 7:7-25, can take place after a person becomes a Christian. In this 'vale of soul-making' conflict is inevitable and necessary. For inner tension can be productive, a spur to moral and spiritual progress. 'When the fight begins within himself, a man's worth something. God stoops o'er his head, Satan looks up between his feet – both tug – he's left, himself, in the middle: the soul *wakes and grows*.'[4] What is true of the fight within is also true of the fight without. As we have seen, the peace, which is the legacy of Christ, does not depend on favourable circumstances. The hymn writer John Newton can say, 'with Christ in the vessel, I smile at the storm'. There are storms on the voyage of life as well as calm seas, and serenity of heart can be ours in all weathers. But not without the guard, the vigilance, the discipline. 'We have peace…let us have peace.'

The discipline of continuing in the peace which God gives has to do primarily with the will, our wills in relationship to the will of God. Christ's peace, his legacy, was the outcome of his perfect union with the Father, of his obedience in all things to the will of God. For us also that is the path to peace. We are restless and anxious because the old self-centred nature is not yet dead. Sometimes it is very much alive. Not only must a Christian keep guard over the impulses that come up from the cellar, the sub-conscious depths, he must also stand as sentry over his personality as a whole. 'Keep your heart with all vigilance; for from it flow the springs of life' (Pr. 4:23). In Hebrew thought the heart is primarily the seat of volition. A man is what he wills. To will in accordance with the will of God disclosed in Christ is to be kept in that peace of God which surpasses any scheme or device of man for giving serenity to his own heart. God's will or self-will; that's the ultimate choice. 'There are only two kinds of people in the end: those who say to God, "Thy will be done", and those to whom God says, in the end: "Thy will be done".'[5] This secret of peace is superbly expressed in the immortal words of Dante, 'In His will is our peace.'[6]

Hindrances and helps to peace

So be on your guard against the enemies of inner peace. Six of the most common are noted here. For each of these hindrances there is a help; for each of these maladies there is a specific remedy.

1. *Sin and confession* An Old Testament prophet, after promising peace to the penitent, describes the restlessness of the impenitent. 'The wicked are like the tossing sea; for it

cannot rest, and its waters toss up mire and dirt. There is no peace, says my God, for the wicked' (Is. 57:19-21). There can be no peaceful co-existence between deliberate sin and the peace of God. No man can have both. When peace is lost through wrong-doing there is only one way to recover it. Turn from sin to God, confess the sin to God, ask for and receive his forgiveness, trusting in the sacrificed-life of his Son, Jesus Christ. 'If we confess our sins, he is just, and may be trusted to forgive our sins, and cleanse us from every kind of wrong...we are being cleansed from every sin by the blood of Jesus his Son' (1 Jn. 1:9, 7 NEB).

2. *Worry and prayer*   One of the most prevalent of our sins is worry, and unless that enemy is being conquered we cannot continue in peace. Jesus taught us not to be anxious about food and clothing, shelter and security. Instead of worrying about the future, we are to carry today's burden only, to give absolute priority to God and to trust him to provide all that is needful (Mt. 6:25-34). We tend to worry when we are afraid, and cannot at the time do anything about the cause of our fear. The antidote to worry is action, and there is always something we can do. Paul links worry with prayer and prayer with peace. 'Have no anxiety about anything, but in everything by prayer and supplication with thanksgiving let your requests be made known to God. And the peace of God, which passes all understanding, will keep your hearts and your minds in Christ Jesus' (Phil. 4:6-7). Is anything worrying you? Tell God all about it, and ask for his help, expressing your gratitude for all that he has already done for you and given you. Then the peace of God will be your guard against all anxiety.

3. *Ambition and contentment*   The desire to get to the top is one of the deepest drives of human nature. It is also the source of much of our disquiet and restlessness. The urge to get on, to achieve, to possess, is the hallmark of our acquisitive society. Not that ambition is necessarily wrong; but it is often corrupted by selfishness. The self-centred desire for possessions and security, for place and power, merits the rebuke of

107

Jeremiah to Baruch, 'Do you seek great things for yourself? Seek them not' (Je. 45:5). The man of relentless ambition is a leech, a blood-sucker, for whom enough is not enough (Pr. 30:15). The antidote is contentment. For this, the Tractarian leader, E. B. Pusey, suggested the following rules. 'Complain of nothing; never compare your lot with that of another; never picture yourself to yourself in any circumstances in which you are not; never dwell on the morrow.'[7] Paul found contentment, not in the self-sufficiency of the Stoic, but in the life and power which came to him from Christ. 'I have learned, in whatever state I am, to be content…I can do all things in him who strengthens me' (Phil. 4:11, 13). Such contentment goes hand in hand with peace.

4. *Over-activity and selectivity* The speed and pressure of life today are a serious threat to inner peace. The temptation is to be over-active, to fill up the hours and days with work and voluntary service, engagements and commitments, hobbies and recreations. The result is an acute shortage of time. To catch up, we hurry and run, hustle and bustle. We become tense, overburdened, frantic. The remedy for over-activity is a wise selectivity. Christ our example didn't rush here and there, trying to do everything in three years. He confined himself to Israel. He healed this person and not that, seized this opportunity and refused that. He got his priorities right. Such a purposeful selectiveness is the friend of poise and peace.

5. *Moods and purpose* Moods are a serious threat; we can lose our peace of mind if we don't master them. A mood is an emotion, not short and intense, but diffused, mild, and of long duration. Some moods are a help (we may be cheerful, optimistic, happy) and others are a hindrance (we may feel resentful, irritable, lustful). Most people are subject at one time or another to the mood commonly known as 'the blues'. In an extreme form it can be dangerous, for what have been called the dreadful d's – despondency, discouragement, depression, despair – can take away our peace. Moods are feelings and our feelings tend to rise and fall like the

temperature-chart of a feverish patient. We should learn to depend, not upon them, but upon will, intention and purpose. In the ministry of Christ, as we have observed, peace and purpose go together. He had a goal and he was persistent. Keeping on keeping on, full constancy of purpose, will carry us through all our moods and keep us in peace.

6. *Negative and positive thinking*   Our thoughts as well as our emotions can be a hindrance to peace. We can get into the habit of entertaining negative thoughts, for example, of remorse for the past, or inferiority about ourselves, of envy and malice towards others, of defeatism concerning our work, of fear for the future. In the long term such thoughts profoundly influence the personality, conscious and unconscious. What a man thinks he tends to become. As the philosopher and emperor Marcus Aurelius put it, 'As are thy habitual thoughts, so will be the character of thy mind, for the soul is dyed the colour of its thought.' The antidote for negative thought is positive thought. Paul, having first assured us that the peace of God will guard our hearts and our thoughts, goes on immediately to say, 'Fill your minds with those things that are good and that deserve praise: things that are true, noble, right, pure, lovely, and honourable' (Phil. 4:8 GNB). We can establish the habit of thinking thoughts that are positive, healthy and happy, loving and kind, confident and encouraging, hopeful and serene. In this connection the practice of memorizing some of the great texts of Scripture, especially those about the peace of God, and of repeating and affirming them, is to be commended. It's one way of staying the mind on God and of being kept in his perfect peace.

Peace between Christians

Peace is three-fold. It is reconciliation, serenity and concord. From our reconciliation with God through Christ there flows not only that inner tranquillity we have just been describing but also fellowship and harmony with others. Peace is corporate. *Shalōm*, we recall, is 'the harmony of a caring community'. It is wholeness, and we are complete when we are knit together in love. Peace is found within the fellowship created and indwelt by the Holy Spirit. It is within the Christian community that the Spirit produces the fruit of peace.

Christ came to make peace between people. Let's take one example of this, especially important in the apostolic age, peace between Jew and Gentile. Only Jews could enter the inner court of the temple at Jerusalem. Between that inner court and the spacious outer court to which the Gentiles were admitted, was a wall. At intervals along that wall were stones bearing an inscription. 'No man of another race is to proceed within the partition and enclosing wall about the sanctuary; and anyone arrested there will have himself to blame for the penalty of death which will be imposed as a consequence.'[8] This wall Paul takes as a symbol of the ancient division and hostility between Jew and Gentile. In the Christian fellowship the barrier has disappeared. 'For he (Christ Jesus) is our peace, who has made us both (Jew and Gentile) one, and has broken down the dividing wall of hostility.' By annulling the Jewish law which caused the enmity, Christ creates one new humanity, within which the old divisions of race and religion are surmounted, 'so making peace' (Eph. 2:14-15). This is a typical example of what Christ has come to do for all mankind. He breaks down the walls that divide, he transforms enemies into friends, he creates the community in which all have the same status as sons of God. 'There is neither Jew nor Greek, there is neither slave nor free, there is neither male nor female; for you are all one in Christ Jesus' (Gal. 3:28).

Peace is like a king. Enthroned in the fellowship it should be allowed to rule and arbitrate. Churches are imperfect communities because they consist of Christians who are imperfect people. So there will be friction and tensions. Differences and disputes are bound to arise. When this happens there must be someone to make the decisions and settle the disputes. The peace which Christ gives, Paul likens to the umpire at the games. 'Let Christ's peace be arbiter in your hearts; to this peace you were called as members of a single body' (Col. 3:15 NEB). The application is both personal and communal. Peace must be allowed to reign in our hearts and over the community. Whenever we have to make decisions or settle disputes, inwardly controlled by the peace which Christ gives, we shall endeavour to preserve peace in the community. That will be the deciding consideration. When we assert our own wills and insist on our own way, the harmony of the community is imperilled. 'In his will is our peace.' That is true of concord as well as of tranquillity, of communal as well as personal peace.

This communal harmony should never be taken for granted. To have it is not necessarily to keep it: it can be lost. Peace has to be maintained and all Christians must be zealous to maintain it. 'Spare no effort to make fast with bonds of peace the unity which the Spirit gives' (Eph. 4:3 NEB). The Spirit creates unity: Christians must maintain it. We must work hard at keeping our relationships in repair, making them fast with the bonds of peace. This applies to the unit of Christian community, the family. It is in the context of marriage and the family that Paul writes, 'God has called us to peace' (1 Cor. 7:15). To this peace God has called each local church, and 'the whole company of Christ's faithful people'. Church history is a sad and tragic story. Christians have found it difficult to live in peace with one another. We still do. A divided church is a contradiction and frustration of God's purpose to unite all things in Christ. Disunity should never be accepted as normal. Through prayer, dialogue and co-operation, we should spare no effort to remove the barriers which divide Christians, and make visible the unity the Spirit gives. We should strive for peace because God wills it, Christ came to make it and the Spirit gives it. The unity of the church, however, is not an end in itself. The church exists for the world, which God in Christ has reconciled to himself. God's people are called to demonstrate and embody that unity which is his purpose for all mankind.

Peace in the world

Christians live in the world and they are called, as far as in them lies, to live peaceably, not only with one another, but with all men. That isn't easy: it requires effort, strenuous and persistent. 'Strive for peace with all men.' 'Seek peace and pursue it' (Heb. 12:14; 1 Pet. 3:11). Writing about our relationships with people outside the church, Paul counsels us not to repay evil for evil, and to respect the convictions and moral standards of the ordinary man. 'So far as it depends upon you, live peaceably with all' (Rom. 12:17-18). If hostility does arise, and it is sometimes inevitable, it must not originate with the Christian. If a Christian is opinionated and dogmatic, or harsh and censorious, or fanatical and aggressive, or smug and self-righteous then he will inevitably alienate and repel those outside the fellowship. On the other hand, the Christian in whose character and conduct the fruits of the Spirit are seen, who is loving and joyful, peaceable and patient, kind and good, loyal, gentle and controlled, will attract and draw like a magnet. He will make friends and make peace.

We are called to make peace, in one of two ways. The barrier to be removed, the alienation to be overcome, may be between you and some other person. In that case, says Jesus, it's up to you to take the initiative, to endeavour to right the wrong relationship (Mt. 18:15). Indeed, your own relationship with God is involved, for you cannot truly worship God unless you are reconciled with your brother. 'So if you are about to offer your gift to God at the altar and there you remember that your brother has something against you, leave your gift there in front of the altar, go at once and make peace with your brother, and then come back and offer your gift to God' (Mt. 5:23-24 GNB). The attempt to put matters right may or may not succeed, but it must be made. The barrier to be removed, however, may be between two other people, or groups of people. Making peace between people who are estranged is a notoriously difficult task, not to be lightly undertaken. It calls for wisdom and understanding, tact and patience, in the counsellor or go-between. It's easy to be a trouble-maker and do the devil's work of dividing; it's hard to be a peace-maker and do God's work of uniting. Yet those who do make peace are blessed; in character they are like God, the supreme maker of peace. 'How blest are the peacemakers; God shall call them his sons' (Mt. 5:9 NEB). The blessing is not on those who love, but on those who make, peace. No Christian should be content to enjoy inner peace: he is called to be an active agent, one who establishes peace in the realm of personal relationships. Like Francis of Assisi he should pray , 'Lord, make me an instrument of thy peace.'

The Christian's concern for peace in the world should not be confined to the sphere of personal relationships. It has economic and social, racial and national dimensions. Problems of poverty, race and war are especially urgent and menacing. There is 'the dividing wall of hostility' between the 'have nots' and the 'haves', between the blacks and the whites, between East and West. Like the dividing wall in the Jewish temple, the Berlin wall is a symbol. The balance of terror, the stock-piling of nuclear weapons, tend to produce a sense of helplessness in the presence of unassailable power. What can Christians do to make peace in such a world?

1. The primary and continuing task of the church is to proclaim to all nations the gospel of reconciliation, to offer to men that peace which God has already made in Christ. It can be known and enjoyed here and now in this world by all who receive God's salvation and do his will (Lk. 2:14).

2. God makes peace through his people's prayers. We are urged by the apostle to pray for all in authority that we 'may lead a quiet and peaceable life' (1 Tim. 2:1-2). We are to keep on asking him 'whose will is to restore all things in his beloved Son, the king of all, to govern the hearts and minds of those in authority, and bring the families of the nations, divided and torn apart by the ravages of sin, to be subject to his most gentle rule.'[9]

3. Remembering the prophetic message that peace is the effect of righteousness, Christians everywhere should strive for economic and social justice. For wherever injustice is set right and justice is done, some of the causes of strife are removed and the cause of peace is advanced.

4. Some Christians are more deeply involved in the world, in the social, industrial and political structures. They are in positions of influence and leadership, and have specialized knowledge and ability. It is their responsibility to do all they can, where they are, to promote justice and peace. All such should be backed by the prayers, the encouragement and the support of all their fellow-Christians in the local church and in the churches. These are some of the ways we can strive for peace in the world. But is it any use striving? Does the Bible promise peace on earth? Is universal peace a mirage?

Peace and hope

The prophets of the Old Testament looked forward to the establishment here on earth of God's kingdom of righteousness and peace. An ideal king of Davidic descent, endowed with the Spirit, would rule with wisdom, justice and might, as God's representative. Nature would be transformed and the wild beasts would live in harmony with domestic animals and with men. Brutality and violence would cease, and all creatures under the sovereignty of God would live at peace (Is. 11:1-9). In those days all nations taught by God and obedient to his word, would transform their weapons of destruction into instruments of fruitfulness. War would no longer be taught to the rising generation and the ordinary man would enjoy peace and security (Mi. 4:1-4). The Messiah would enter Jerusalem, triumphant and victorious, riding on an ass, symbol of peace. He would destroy armaments, restore the ancient kingdom of David and secure peace among all nations (Zc. 9:9-10). These prophetic hopes had to confront the stubborn fact of evil. From the first century BC onwards the stream divides. Some, convinced that this world was too corrupt for the kingdom to be set up here, looked for the fulfilment of God's purpose beyond history in a new creation. Others continued to hope for a terrestrial kingdom of limited duration. This intermediate kingdom, the reign of the Messiah on earth, would be followed by the transcendent and eternal kingdom of God.

This conception of a terrestrial kingdom, limited in time, appears in the book of Revelation, in John's picture of the millennium, the thousand years' reign of Christ with his saints on earth (Rev. 20:1-10). This millennial hope has had a profound influence on the minds of men, both within and outside the church. It's a mistake to take John's picture literally, and to interpret it as a chronological record of successive events. He is not symbolizing a period in the distant future, but a process which is going on all the time. Christ is reigning and will reign on the earth, and the devil and the powers of evil are always breaking loose and re-capturing what has been won by Christ and his people. These two processes are depicted in the two parts of the picture – verses 4 to 6, and verses 7 to 10 of chapter 20.

The cause of God will be vindicated, not only in some transcendent realm, but also here on earth. Wrongs done on earth will be redressed on earth. Christ lived, suffered and died here on earth; he will reign on earth. Though concealed and incomplete, his kingdom of justice and peace is a present reality. We may legitimately strive for its extension and hope for its fuller manifestation here on earth.

The weeds as well as the wheat, however, are growing in the field of the world; there is a progress in evil as well as in good. The victories gained for justice and peace can be lost. Satan is let loose from his prison and rallies the powers of evil. It keeps on happening. 'The powers of evil have a defence in depth, which enables them constantly to summon reinforcements from beyond the frontiers of man's knowledge and control. However far human society progresses, it can never, while this world lasts, reach the point where it is invulnerable to such attacks.'[10] We must not therefore look for the full realization of our hope on earth, but in heaven. 'The kingdom of God cannot be established in this earthly historical world because it is incompatible with two factors which are inherent in the latter: with the power of sin still operative even in the regenerate, and with the power of death.'[11]

We don't have to choose between these two hopes. It doesn't make sense to cease striving for peace on earth because we know that there can be perfect peace only in heaven. To say, as some Christians do, that there will always be wars and rumours of wars, and that we cannot hope for peace on earth, is to ignore what has been done in the past and can be done in the future. Through his people and all men of goodwill, the hidden but reigning Christ has often prevented strife and kept the peace. These victories, temporary and precarious, are a manifestation of his reign. What is more, the fruits of justice and peace are never really lost. Even if they are lost on earth they are taken up into the eternal kingdom. That is another facet of the truth in the symbol of the millennium. Just as the resurrection of the body means that the experience of the individual on earth is taken up into the eternal kingdom, so the experience of the human race, the worthy achievements and victories of mankind, are taken up into the kingdom which fulfils and transcends history. 'They shall bring into it (the new Jerusalem) the glory and the honour of the nations' (Rev. 21:26). The values and treasures of earth are taken into heaven. Living, as we do, in the overlap of the two ages, the eternal kingdom is also here and now. We possess already the first instalment of the final reality, the kingdom of God which is 'righteousness and peace and joy in the Holy Spirit' (Rom. 14:17). Righteousness and peace are the traditional characteristics of the messianic age. They are the titles of Christ, the King of Righteousness, the King of Peace. He is King of Salem, Jerusalem. Salem, like *shalōm*, means peace (Heb. 7:1-2). We shall find perfect peace in the heavenly Jerusalem, the city of the King of Peace.

Notes for chapter six

1. J. V. Taylor, *Enough is Enough* (S.C.M., 1975), p.41.
2. *Christian Melodies*, 1858.
3. B. H. Streeter and A. J. Appasamy, *The Sadhu* (Macmillan).
4. Robert Browning, *Bishop Blougham's Apology*.
5. C. S. Lewis, *The Great Divorce* (Macmillan, 1965), p.69.
6. Dante, *Divine Comedy: Paradiso,* III, 85.
7. Quoted by M. W. Tileston, *Daily Strength for Daily Needs* (Methuen, 1904), p.144.
8. A translation of the Greek inscription on one of those stones, found on the temple site in 1871, now in a museum in Istanbul.
9. Collect for the 16th Sunday after Pentecost (*Alternative Service Book*).
10. G. B. Caird, *The Revelation of St. John the Divine* (Adam and Charles Black, 1966), p.257.
11. Emil Brunner, *Eternal Hope* (Lutterworth, 1954), p.76.

7 Patience

Patience and endurance

> Patience is a virtue, possess it if you can:
> Seldom in a woman, and never in a man.

When I was a child, those lines were often quoted to me by my mother. They may be taken as an example of male sex discrimination in reverse, since they affirm the slight superiority of women to men! What they are intended to do, however, is to draw attention to the rarity of patience in both sexes. Fortunately, patience isn't as rare as all that, but it is a virtue often lacking in otherwise virtuous people. I have often studied and discussed the nine fruits of the Spirit with other Christians, using the list as a standard for self-examination. For most of us it's when we come to the fourth in the list, patience, that we are most painfully aware of our failure to live in accordance with the character of Christ. In the western world not only is patience rare, it is also unpopular. Perhaps patience, the virtue, and patient, a person undergoing medical treatment, are somehow vaguely associated in our minds. Patience, we suppose, is entirely passive, allowing ourselves to be acted upon. We prefer to act. All the same it is probably true to say that, at home, at work, and in all our personal relationships, more sheer misery is caused by impatience than by any other moral weakness. The rare and unpopular virtue is indispensable.

In the Greek New Testament there are several words which have reference to a person's ability to cope with difficult people or with adverse circumstances. The two most important of them are translated as *patience* and *endurance*. The Greek word for the fourth fruit of the Spirit is *makrothymia*, translated *longsuffering* in the Authorized Version, and *patience* in all the later versions. Like the word *forbearance*, patience has to do primarily with people, with our response to them when they are difficult, trying or provocative. 'Put on then...patience, forbearing one another' (Col. 3:12-13). It's that quality of character which enables a person to hold out for a time, maybe for a long time, before giving way to either passion or anger. The old English word, no longer current, *longanimity* very well describes this tenacious state of mind. Patience is the capacity to be 'long-minded', to delay making a response to provocative people.

The other Greek word, *hypomonē*, translated *endurance* or *steadfastness*, has to do primarily with circumstances rather than with people. He exercises *hypomonē* 'who under a great siege of trials, bears up and does not lose heart or courage'.[1] Endurance is both passive and active. It is acceptance and submission, and it is perseverance and steadfastness under trial. Timothy, Paul's companion in travel, had seen both patience and endurance in the character and conduct of the pioneer missionary. 'You have observed...my patience... what persecutions I endured' (2 Tim. 3:10-11). Timothy had seen two qualities which are akin. Paul's patience in dealing with difficult people, and his endurance in adverse circumstances, opposition and persecution in Pisidian Antioch, Lystra and Iconium. We are concerned in this chapter with both these qualities of character.

The patience of Christ

The patience and steadfastness of Jesus are to be seen in his portraits, the gospels. At the outset of his ministry he was tempted by the devil in the wilderness. He was tempted to be impatient. All three temptations have reference to his vocation as Messiah and Servant. He was tempted to aim at quick results, by using the power entrusted to him to meet his own needs; by spectacular supernatural display; by taking the military way to worldly power (Mt. 4:1-11). All three suggestions he rejected and continued to reject, choosing the slow and arduous way of establishing the kingdom, the way of teaching and service, of suffering and sacrifice. This strategy of patient love is to be seen in his work as a preacher and teacher. He taught and trained his slow and obtuse disciples with patience. He made use of parables, he repeated his lessons, he explained his meaning, he disclosed the truth in stages, as they were able to receive it.

In the parables of the sower, the mustard seed and the patient husbandman, the end is contrasted with the beginning (Mk. 4:1-9, 26-32). The great comes from the small, the bountiful harvest from the scattering of the seeds. The mission of Jesus and his small group of disciples had an inconspicuous beginning; it would have a glorious consummation when the kingdom came with power. Between the inconspicuous beginning and the glorious end it was necessary to work and wait with patience and assurance. Jesus, the preacher and teacher, sower of the seed of the word, did not look for quick results; he was prepared to wait for the fruit of his labours. Not before his death, but beyond it, he expected a great harvest (Jn. 12:24). He was patient with people, with his dull disciples, with the fickle crowds that flocked to him for the wrong reasons, with the sick who pressed upon him for healing, with his enemies who tried to trap him in his talk. On occasions we see his patience strained almost to breaking point, as when he cried out, 'How unbelieving you people are! How long must I stay with you? How long do I have to put up with you?' (Mk. 9:19 GNB).

It is, above all, in scenes connected with his passion and death that the patience and steadfastness of Christ are fully revealed. He was patient with people. Unjustly condemned as deserving death by the Jewish council, 'some began to spit on him, and to cover his face, and to strike him, saying to him, "Prophesy!" And the guards received him with blows' (Mk. 14:65). Inside the praetorium, the Roman soldiers clothed him in a purple robe, crowned him with thorns, struck his head with a military cane, spat on him and knelt before him in mock homage (Mk. 15:16-19). What was his response to all these provocative people? Peter tells us. 'When he was insulted, he did not answer back with an insult; when he suffered, he did not threaten, but placed his hopes in God, the righteous Judge' (1 Pet. 2:23 GNB). He also faced adverse circumstances, the extremity of physical, mental and spiritual suffering, accompanied by stinging indignity and utter disgrace, with resolution and steadfastness. 'Jesus...endured the cross, making light of its disgrace' (Heb. 12:2 NEB). Paul draws attention to this virtue of steadfastness or endurance in the character of the Lord Jesus, and prays that Christians, through their commitment to him, may possess this same grace. 'May the Lord direct your hearts to the love of God and to the steadfastness of Christ' (2 Thes. 3:5).

Waiting for the Lord

Patience is a virtue which must operate in three dimensions, in three relationships. We need to be patient with God, with other people and with ourselves. We shall look at these three aspects in turn. That we have to learn to be patient with God will come as no surprise to readers of the Bible. The servants of God were often tempted to be impatient with him. Prophets and psalmists sometimes complain bitterly and express forcefully their impatience with God. That's because he seems to be so slow in doing things, or he fails to do them at all. They pray to God; they receive no answer to their prayers. They appeal for help; the help is not forthcoming. In urgent need they cry out to God for immediate action; they are disappointed. 'I have cried desperately for help, but still it does not come' (Ps. 22:1 GNB). Individuals bring to God pressing problems and receive no light on them. As a nation, oppressed by enemies or exiled in a distant land, they wait in vain for God to redress their fortune. At times, complaints and protests become rude and impertinent. 'Wake up, Lord! Why are you asleep? Rouse yourself! Don't reject us for ever!' (Ps. 44:23 GNB). Time and again his exasperated people call on God to wake up, to bestir himself, to get on with it!

Our impatience with God is bound up with our misunderstanding of time. God's time is not our time. We are in time;

the eternal God is not in time. Unlike us, the Creator of the world does not measure time by the things he has made, the phases of the moon, the rotation of the earth and its journey round the sun. So then, we must not measure his tempo by our days and months, our years and centuries. Peter refers to the sceptics who had lost faith in the promise of the coming of the Lord because his coming had been so long delayed. He assures his readers that God has a different time-scale. 'But do not ignore this one fact, beloved, that with the Lord one day is as a thousand years, and a thousand years as one day. The Lord is not slow about his promise as some count slowness' (2 Pet. 3:8-9). God appears to be slow; in fact, says Peter, he is providing men with an ample opportunity to repent. Of God's tempo we must say three things: God is not slow; God is not in a hurry; God is deliberate.

God is not slow, but his purposes often seem to us to be slow-paced. That is why we must learn to wait on the Lord, believing that he will act in his own way, at his own time. When the prophet Habakkuk received no satisfying answer to the problem of suffering and oppression, he was told to wait for it. 'For still the vision awaits its time; it hastens to the end – it will not lie. If it seem slow, wait for it; it will surely come, it will not delay' (Hab. 2:3). God's purposes mature slowly, but surely. The vision given to the prophet will, in due time, flower, ripen, come to fulfilment. Impatient men demand immediate answers to perplexing problems; usually, the meaning of events can be seen only after a long period of time. We may have to wait a long time to see the meaning of some of the events within our own life-span, and only in the clear light of eternity will the complete answer be given to some of the problems that perplex us.

Waiting for the Lord, however, does not mean idle inactivity, dull listlessness, lethargic resignation. 'My soul waits for the Lord more than watchmen for the morning' (Ps. 130:6). Like men looking for the dawn after a long night, we are to wait in anticipation and hope. We are to look eagerly for the comings and the actions of the Lord, in creation and history, through people and events. That was the message of Isaiah to the exiles in Babylon. They were despondent and hopeless. After more than forty years in captivity they had come to the conclusion that God had forgotten all about them. The prophet sees that God is about to liberate them, using Cyrus of Persia as his instrument. He calls upon them to turn to God with expectaton. Lord of all time, unlimited in power and wisdom, he is the unfailing source of renewal and strength to all those who wait patiently for him. 'They who wait for the Lord shall renew their strength, they shall mount up with wings like eagles, they shall run and not be weary, they shall walk and not faint' (Is. 40:31).

Patience with people

We must also learn to be patient with all the members of the Christian community. Paul had the fellowship in mind, when he wrote 'love is patient' (1 Cor. 13:4). Patience is an aspect of caring; it's one of the colours in the spectrum of love. It's the way in which a loving person responds to, and deals with, trying and difficult people. In this respect the grace of patience differs from the pagan virtue. Christian patience is not a virtue of the self-sufficient individual, cultivated to perfect his own character. Its context is the community. The apostle appeals to Christians within the church, to relate to one another 'with patience, forbearing one another in love' (Eph. 4:2). As 'God's chosen ones, holy and beloved', three words descriptive of Israel, the people of God in the Old Testament, they are to put on the garments of patience and reciprocal forbearance (Col. 3:12-13). The church on earth is not an ideal community; it's not comprised of perfect people. To imagine that it is, or should be, is to court disillusionment. Because all Christians are imperfect and the church includes difficult people, Paul's appeal to the leaders applies to every member of the church, 'Be patient with them all' (1 Thes. 5:14).

Beyond the Christian fellowship there is even greater need and opportunity to exercise patience in our personal relationships. Those who live or learn, work or play together, husbands and wives, parents and children, brothers and sisters, teachers and pupils, employers and workers, friends and neighbours, can, and often do, irritate and provoke one another. It's in these relationships that we need prosaic or humdrum, rather than heroic, patience. For in the course of an ordinary day it's the little, rather than the big, things, which try our patience. Many a person who has shown fortitude in facing a major challenge, accident, sickness, redundancy, bereavement, has succumbed to the petty irritations of daily life, a late train, a wet washing day, a noisy child, an inquisitive neighbour. God provides us with plenty of raw material for developing the virtue of patience, the untidy son or daughter, the guest with bad table manners, the neighbour who borrows without returning, the typist who is habitually late, the person in the next pew who sings out of tune, the bore who monopolizes the conversation. The list could be extended indefinitely!

There are three things in particular which need to be handled with patience: untimely interruptions, negative criticism and harsh words. Often, in the course of a day, because of the intrusion of others, we are not allowed to get on with our work or with the enjoyment of our leisure. Sit down to write a letter or to prepare an address, and the telephone keeps on ringing. Set aside an evening to watch your favourite programme on TV or to read a new book, and there is a succession of callers. We can discipline ourselves to accept these untimely interruptions with patience and courtesy, making ourselves totally available to others. Jesus retreated to the other side of the Lake of Galilee for quiet and relaxation. His privacy was invaded by a crowd. He was moved with compassion; he welcomed them, taught them and fed them (Mk. 6:30-34).

Our natural reaction to negative criticism is resentment. We become angry when people draw attention to our imperfections, faults and failures. Either we attempt to justify ourselves or we criticize our critics even more trenchantly. Instead of making a hasty response at the time, it is better to go away and think calmly over what has been said. If it is untrue, we can resolve to ignore it; if there is some truth in it, we can profit from it. For our critics can be our best friends; whatever their intentions, they can help us to recognize and correct our defects. 'One Sunday, after I had preached what

I thought was a good sermon, one of my critics confronted me. "In this Church", he said coldly, "sermons are limited to twenty-five minutes. You ran two minutes over." I managed to keep my temper till I got home. Then I blew up.' Fortunately that preacher, Norman Vincent Peale, had a wise father, who taught him how to accept criticism with creative patience, and thus to profit from it.[2]

'A mild answer turns away wrath, sharp words stir up anger' (Pr. 15:1 jb). Harsh words hurt; they kindle the fire of anger. Under the impulse of that anger, the person who has been hurt responds to harsh words with harsh words. So there is a dog-fight. It requires great calmness and patience to respond to a harsh word with a gentle and kindly answer, but that is the way in which a quarrel can be averted. Gracious words are powerful and effective; tempers cool, wrath is turned away, dissension is avoided. Why have miserable and damaging quarrels when, as Robert Louis Stevenson said, 'With a little more patience and a little less temper, a gentler and wiser method might be found in every case'?

Anger and bad temper

It's when we are angry that we find it most difficult to be patient with people. As the word *makrothymia* indicates, patience operates in the context of anger. *Makros* means *long*, and *thymos* means *anger*. Patience is the prolonged restraint of anger. It's to be long-tempered rather than short-tempered. The patient person doesn't fly off the handle! Instead of allowing anger to flare up quickly, it is held in check, maybe for a long time. Anger is not necessarily wrong, nor should it always be held in restraint. There is a tendency nowadays to assume that anger is always bad. The word *temper*, for example, is associated with the word *bad*, although a person may have a congenial temper or some other agreeable disposition of mind. Anger can be excellent; it is a characteristic of God himself. It's true that God is 'slow to anger', but he does become angry. There is a divine impatience with evil. God doesn't always restrain his anger, and the servants of God should not always restrain theirs. Of the stubborn Israelites who refused to listen to God's word, Jeremiah says, 'Your anger against them burns in me too, Lord, and I can't hold it in any longer' (Je. 6:11 GNB). Jesus was angry sometimes (*e.g.* Mk. 3:5; 10:14; 11:15).

A wise man once exclaimed, 'Anger is one of the sinews of the soul; he who lacks it hath a maimed mind.' To be unmoved by the evils done to others is a sign of moral weakness. The re-birth of indignation in the presence of selfishness, cruelty and oppression, is one of the great needs of our time. Abraham Lincoln was angry, very angry, when he said of slavery, 'If ever I get a chance to hit that thing, I'll hit it hard.' The two kinds of anger, the good and the bad, are to be distinguished by their centre. Good anger is other-people centred; bad anger is self-centred. Indignation is consecrated anger. It is kindled by wrong done to others, and is a sign of concern for their welfare. Bad temper always has a self-reference. Most of us are still, to some extent, self-centred. Therefore wrongs, real or imaginary, done to us by trying and difficult people, provoke us to outbursts of irritability, temper or vindictiveness. In the light of this distinction between indignation and bad temper, we may have to confess with George Matheson, 'There are times when I do well to be angry, but I have mistaken the times.'[3]

There are two failures which can be overcome by the exercise of the virtue of patience: the angry outburst and the angry mood. When tempted to an outburst of anger, make a habit of delaying your response. Thomas Jefferson gave this advice, 'When angry, count ten before you speak; if very angry, count a hundred.' During the delay, the anger cools, the fire dies down. After the delay the angry man may decide not to say or do anything, or he may then express his anger in appropriate words or actions. More dangerous than the flare-up is the angry mood. For the outcome of lingering anger may be the harboured grudge, the cherished resentment. Concerning the angry mood, Paul gives excellent advice. 'If you are angry, do not let anger lead you into sin; do not let sunset find you still nursing it; leave no loop-hole for the devil' (Eph. 4:26 NEB). Never carry over your anger from one day to another. How many marriages, how many personal relationships, would have been saved from disruption if this wise and practical counsel had been heeded!

Patience with ourselves

We have to learn to be patient, not only with God and with other people but also with ourselves. Since the Lord is patient with us, we must be patient with ourselves. This is not just a plea for complacency. To accept ourselves as we are is not to stay as we are. Progress is possible; but it is slow. Christian character is not created and shaped by the Holy Spirit in a hurry. That truth is implicit in the picture-language Paul uses about the fruit or the harvest of the Spirit. There is a necessary and lengthy period of time between spring and autumn, between the seed and the fruit, between the sowing and the harvest. 'First the blade, then the ear, then the full grain in the ear' (Mk. 4:28). The process cannot be hurried. We must not try to outpace the Holy Spirit. Brother Lawrence complains of a young woman he was counselling, 'She seems to me full of goodwill, but she would go faster than grace. One does not become holy all at once.'

Being patient with oneself means acceptance, moderation and relaxation. Since God has accepted us just as we are, we must accept ourselves just as we are. On the walls of the sanctuary of the Jewish temple 'every cherub had two faces', the face of a lion and the face of a man (Ezk. 41:18-19). Each one of us is a strange mixture of the animal and the human, the sensuous and the spiritual. We must recognize and accept our total human nature. 'If we are to know peace and freedom from the war within, the unpleasant as well as the pleasant things must be accepted. The trouble with some people is that they want to attain perfection all at once, and so they feel continually frustrated and depressed because they cannot accept human failings and limitations.'[4]

Any resolutions we make about progress in character and conduct should be modest, not magnificent. Because of the frailty of our human nature, we should avoid rigorism, the making of impossible moral demands on ourselves. 'People who love themselves aright', says Fénelon, 'set to work patiently, not exacting more than is practicable under present circumstances from themselves any more than from others, and not being disheartened because perfection is not attainable in a day.' There is a striving, an effort required of us, if we are to make progress in the Christian life, but it should be set in the larger context of trusting and resting, of relaxation and tranquillity. The anonymous author of the following prayer was learning to be patient with himself. 'Slow me down, Lord. Remind me each day of the fable of the hare and the tortoise, that I may know that the race is not always for the swift; that there is more to life than increasing its speed. Let me look upward into the branches of the towering oak and know that it grew great and strong because it grew slowly and well.'

Wait, persist and endure

Patience has to do with our desires and our activities and with the things that happen to us, especially with adverse events. As described at the beginning of this chapter, this particular aspect of patience is best described by the Greek word *hypomonē*, steadfastness, constancy, endurance. It's the capacity to wait, to accept delay, to hold out, to keep right on to the end of the road. Three aspects will be described, waiting, perseverance, endurance.

Patience is the ability to wait for the satisfaction of desire and for the reward of labour. In the House of the Interpreter, Bunyan's pilgrim, Christian, saw two children. 'The name of the eldest was Passion, and the name of the other Patience. Passion seemed to be much discontented; but Patience was very quiet. Then Christian asked, "What is the reason of the discontent of Passion?" The Interpreter answered, "The Governor of them would have him stay for his best things till the beginning of the next year; but he will have all now; but Patience is willing to wait".' Have all now. One of our big banks makes the alluring offer to 'take the waiting out of wanting'. Patience declines the offer. Rather than enjoy unearned benefits now, and pay for them later on, patience prefers to work for them first and to wait for the ensuing reward. There are, of course, some things (*e.g.* a house) for which we cannot wait until we have paid for them. On the other hand, to acquire *luxuries* on hire-purchase, to spend money which has been neither given nor earned, is indefensible. More seriously, to demand sex before the commitment of marriage is characteristic of the person who 'will have all now'. It has been truly said that when we do right we have the trouble first and the pleasure later: when we do wrong we have the pleasure first and the trouble later.

Patience is also the ability to keep on keeping on. Persistence is one of the great secrets of achievement. A man fleeing from his enemies discovered this when he took refuge in a ruined building. 'Desiring to divert my mind from my hopeless condition, I fixed my eyes on an ant that was carrying a grain of corn larger than itself up a high wall. I numbered the efforts it made to accomplish this object. The grain fell sixty-nine times to the ground; but the insect persevered, and the seventieth time it reached the top.' The ant succeeded at the seventieth attempt. Edison is said to have failed over three thousand times before he succeeded in making an effective filament for the electric light bulb. We need this same perseverance in our voluntary work. Anyone who gives a service is almost certain at times to meet with set-backs, discouragements and disappointments. It may take longer to carry through a project than we had supposed at the outset. There are delays, or there are few, if any, results. The impatient person gives up; the dogged person carries on. The pioneer missionary, William Carey, said to his nephew, 'I can plod. That is my only genius. I can persevere in any definite pursuit. To this I owe everything.'[5] It's the plodders, in the long run, who do most for their fellow men and for their Lord.

'Be patient in tribulation' (Rom. 12:12). Endurance is the ability to face opposition and persecution without breaking down or giving in. Paul praises the Christians of Thessalonica for their constancy in persecution. 'We ourselves boast of you in the churches of God for your steadfastness and faith in all your persecutions and in the afflictions which you are enduring' (2 Thes. 1:4). The Christians of Asia were severely persecuted during the reign of Domitian. John the elder was banished to 'the isle called Patmos', and in Jesus he shared with them 'the tribulation and the kingdom and the patient endurance'. In his flaming manifesto of defiance, John issues a call 'for the endurance of the saints', and promises eternal life to those who keep Christ's 'word of patient endurance', *i.e.* endurance as taught and practised by Christ (Rev. 1:9; 3:10; 13:10). For it was Jesus himself, after forewarning his disciples of the coming tribulations and persecutions, who gave the assurance and promise, 'But he who endures to the end will be saved' (Mt. 24:13). In the New Testament, patience is linked with hope, *the* hope, the blessed hope of the Advent (Rom. 12:12; 1 Thes. 1:3). We can wait, and keep on, and endure, because of what is coming, or rather, because of *who* is coming. 'Be patient, therefore, brethren, until the coming of the Lord. Behold, the farmer waits for the precious fruit of the earth, being patient over it until it receives the early and the late rain. You also be patient. Establish your hearts, for the coming of the Lord is at hand…Behold, we call those happy who were steadfast' (Jas. 5:7-8, 11).

Notes for chapter seven

1. R. C. Trench, *Synonyms of the New Testament* (Macmillan, 1854).
2. N. V. Peale, *Readers Digest,* June 1972.
3. I owe this, and the previous quotation, on page 126, to H. E. Fosdick, *The Manhood of the Master* (S.C.M., 1918).
4. E. White, *Christian Life and the Unconscious* (Hodder and Stoughton, 1954), pp.159-160.
5. S. Pearce Carey, *William Carey* (Hodder and Stoughton, 1923), p.23.

8 Kindness

The most important thing in life

Kindness, the fifth of the fruits of the Spirit, is the most popular virtue. The average man, whether he is a Christian or not, sets a high price label on it. Indeed, this high valuation of kindness often leads people to make foolish and untenable claims for it. 'All this poor old world needs to put it right is a bit of kindness. If we were all to speak the encouraging word, lend a hand, help lame dogs over stiles, be kind to children, old folk and the sick, then all would be well.' In those countries which have a Christian background and heritage, there is a widespread tendency to use the words *Christian* and *kind* as synonymous. 'She's a real Christian' means 'she's a very kind person'. This, of course, is confused thinking; for there are many kind people who are not Christians, just as, unfortunately, there are some Christians who are not kind. Yet this popular judgment, confused though it is, may well be based on the insight and conviction that kindness is of supreme importance.

Prophets and poets share that conviction. Micah, in an oracle which has been called 'the Magna Carta of the prophetic religion', includes kindness to people as one of the three essentials the Lord requires of man. 'He has showed you, O man, what is good; and what does the Lord require of you but to do justice, and to love kindness, and to walk humbly with your God?' (Mi. 6:8). The poet William Wordsworth refers to this virtue as:

> That best portion of a good man's life,
> His little, nameless, unremembered acts
> Of kindness and of love.[1]

Amid all that is superficial and transient in life, kindness, like the everlasting hills, endures.

> Life is mostly froth and bubble,
> Two things stand like stone,
> Kindness in another's trouble,
> Courage in your own.[2]

The Russian author, Y. Yevtushenko, when he was fifteen, joined a geological expedition to Siberia as a labourer. One day, utterly wretched and vermin-infested, he ran off into the steppes and jumped into an abandoned dig. There he was discovered by a young peasant woman who joined him in the pit. 'She pulled my hands away from my face. Intensely blue eyes between long black lashes looked at me with a warm kindness which is much better than pity.' She took him home, gave him a bath, steamed his lousy clothes, spoke to him encouraging words, put him to bed. 'I shall never forget her. Ever since then I have known that if all the values in this world are more or less questionable, the most important thing in life is kindness.'[3] Confirmation of this high valuation of kindness is to be found in our Lord's parable of the Last Judgment. 'I was hungry and you gave me food, I was thirsty and you gave me drink, I was a stranger and you welcomed me, I was naked and you clothed me, I was sick and you visited me, I was in prison and you came to me' (Mt. 25:35-36). Not that Jesus is here teaching salvation by good works. Far from taking a stand on them, those here accepted for eternal life are not even aware of their deeds of kindness! We are saved by grace through faith. Genuine faith, however, is 'faith active in love' (Gal. 5:6 NEB). The righteous in the parable respond to Jesus Christ who is present (though hidden) in his needy brethren, with love. Now since faith and love are inseparable, in the response of love, faith is implicit. The one and only criterion of judgment is our response to

Christ. Without excluding faith, which is insisted upon elsewhere (*e.g.* Mt. 10:32), the emphasis here is upon love. The performance of acts of mercy and kindness is of paramount importance in the eyes of Christ because these acts are evidence of a genuine relationship to him.

Kindnesses: small or great

In literature and in life, kindness is often associated with little things, as in the quotation above from Wordsworth, 'his little…acts of kindness'. It is these which make up the good man's life. Not every day brings the demand for great and costly deeds, but if we are sensitive and alert we can recognize and seize opportunities to perform little acts of kindness. Like a beam of sunshine on a cloudy day any one of these can brighten the life of the recipient of the kindness. They can also have a cumulative effect out of all proportion to the act itself. As Julia Carney expresses it in the children's hymn:

> Little deeds of kindness, little words of love
> Help to make earth happy, like the heaven above.

Jesus emphasized the significance of these little deeds of mercy and helpfulness. To give a thirsty traveller a cup of cold water (a proverbial expression for a minor kindness) is no small thing in the sight of God and will not go unrewarded (Mt. 10:42). To speak a word of encouragement; to give to someone in need; to lend to a neighbour; to telephone or to write to one who is in sorrow; to visit the sick or the aged; to befriend a lonely person; to lend a hand to a harassed friend, there are a hundred and one little ways to be kind to others.

On the other hand, if more occasionally, a great kindness may be required of us, a big demand may be made on our time, energy and resources. Here are two examples, one from the Bible, the other from the story of the church. The prophet Jeremiah was cast into a deep waterless cistern by his enemies. They left him to die. Then Ebed-melech, an Ethiopian servant in the palace of Zedekiah, went to the king and pleaded for the life of the prophet. Risking unpopularity and perhaps even death, to save the life of a condemned man, was itself a great act of kindness. When his request was granted, Ebed-melech's courage was matched by his considerateness. He padded with 'old rags and worn-out clothes' the ropes with which he, and three helpers, drew the prophet out of the mud in which he had sunk, lest they should chafe his armpits. His great act of kindness was done in a kindly way (Je. 38:1-13). The Frenchman, Vincent de Paul, used to visit and assist convicts who had been condemned to work in the galleys. He met a young convict who was broken-hearted at the thought of his wife and children left destitute. Vincent prevailed with the officer in charge of the gang to let him take his place. Set free, the young convict returned to his family. Incognito, Vincent worked for several weeks in chains, with the rest of the gang, until it was discovered who he was. Then he was released. That was no small kindness.

The opportunity for the kind deed, whether small or great, does not always recur. Unless it is seized there and then it may be lost for ever. On one occasion, Jesus drew the attention of his disciples to the importance of recognizing and seizing the non-recurring opportunity for kindness. A few days before his death, Mary of Bethany anointed the feet of Jesus with very costly ointment. Judas complained at the waste: the ointment should have been sold, and the money given to the poor. In reply, Jesus pointed out that the poor are always with us, and we can help them at any time. But Mary had done 'a beautiful thing'. She had seized an opportunity, *which would never recur*, of expressing her devotion to the Saviour (Mk. 14:3-9; Jn. 12:1-7). 'This would be a so much lovelier world if there were more people like this woman, who acted on her impulse of love, because she knew in her heart of hearts that if she did not do it then, she would never do it at all.'[4] When I was at school, my class had to memorize the words attributed to the Quaker, Stephen Grellet. I wish I had always heeded the wise warning. 'I expect to pass through this world but once; any good thing therefore that I can do, or any kindness that I can show to any fellow-creature, let me do it now; let me not defer or neglect it, for I shall not pass this way again.'

Kindness: ordinary and extraordinary

It is a matter of observation, and should be a cause of thankfulness, that kindness is not the monopoly of Christians. When their ship was driven aground in a storm, Paul, Luke and Aristarchus, together with some two hundred and seventy-three other people, escaped to the island of Malta by swimming or by clinging to the flotsam and jetsam of the wrecked and disintegrating ship. Soaked, exhausted and wretched, they received an unexpectedly warm welcome. 'The natives showed us unusual kindness, for they kindled a fire and welcomed us all, because it had begun to rain and was cold' (Acts 28:2). The 'barbarous people' (AV) of Malta were not Christians; but acting upon the inclinations and impulses of their own good nature, they showed unusual kindness to those who were in distress. Luke, the author, recognized ungrudgingly this great kindness of the pagans. Christians should be glad and grateful whenever they see kindness in those who do not belong to Christ.

This is not to deny, however, that there is a distinctive kindness, the grace of kindness, the fruit of the Spirit, given to those who belong to the fellowship of the Spirit. This new kindness, brought into the world by Jesus Christ, was, and should always be, distinctive of the Christian and the Christian community. 'One of the most glorious features of early Christianity was that it introduced a new kindliness into the world – kindliness to little children by which infant exposure was condemned and eventually made a criminal offence; kindliness to the poor and destitute and plague-stricken; kindliness to woman who was given her rightful place in society; kindliness to the common slave who was not treated as a being of inferior clay but as a brother man; kindliness to men of alien race who were deemed fellow-members of the family of God; kindliness that led in due course to the abolition of gladiatorial combats.'[5] It is instructive to study this change from callousness to kindness in the case of a single individual. When Paul and Silas, having been beaten with rods in the market place of Philippi, were handed over to the jailer, he put them in the inner prison and fastened their feet in the stocks. The backs of the two apostles were bruised and bleeding, but the jailer couldn't have cared less. But when he responded to the gospel and put his trust in the Lord Jesus for salvation, there was a significant change. 'He took them the same hour of the night, and washed their wounds' (Acts 16:33). 'Genuine conversion always leads to the display of a kindlier spirit towards men.'[6] There are four aspects of the distinctive kindness, as we see it in God, and in the people of God.

The kindness of God

David and Jonathan made a covenant of friendship. Their pledge of love and loyalty was to include their descendants. 'The Lord shall be between me and you, and between my descendants and your descendants, for ever' (1 Sa. 20:42). Long after the death of his friend Jonathan in battle, King David remembered his pledge. He sent for Ziba, a servant of the house of Saul, and questioned him. 'Is there not still some one of the house of Saul, that I may show the kindness of God to him?' Ziba informed the king that there was still one surviving son of Jonathan, a cripple, Mephibosheth. David sent for him, and said to him, 'I will show you kindness for the sake of your father Jonathan, and I will restore to you all the land of Saul your father; and you shall eat at my table always' (2 Sa. 9:3,7). In this story, the kindness shown by a king to a cripple, in the discharge of covenant obligations, is called 'the kindness of God'.

The English phrase 'the kindness of God' is a translation of the Hebrew word *chesed*. Following the example of Coverdale, this Hebrew word is often translated *lovingkindness* in the Authorized Version of the Bible. In the Revised Standard Version it is almost always translated *steadfast love*. *Chesed* is love plus loyalty, and presupposes the existence of a bond or covenant between two or more parties. The word is often used in conjunction with or as a parallel to the word *faithfulness* (Ps. 36:5). *Chesed* is faithful love, steadfast love, bonded love, covenant love. Its source is God; its sphere is the people with whom God has made a covenant. Like the loyal love of

David which continued beyond the death of Jonathan, the kindness of God for the people of the covenant lasts for ever. 'For the mountains shall depart, and the hills be removed; but my kindness shall not depart from thee, neither shall the covenant of my peace be removed, saith the Lord that hath mercy on thee' (Is. 54:10 AV).

In the fulness of time this everlasting kindness of God was seen and embodied in the life and death of Jesus Christ, the Saviour of mankind, the Mediator of the new covenant. 'When the goodness and loving kindness of God our Saviour appeared, he saved us, not because of deeds done by us in righteousness, but in virtue of his own mercy' (Tit. 3:4-5). Here Paul describes the distinctive aspect of the kindness of God in Christ. God deals with men irrespective of their merits or deserts; he deals with them simply on the ground of his own unmerited kindness. The Greek word for the fifth fruit of the Spirit is *chrēstotēs*. Here we have the precise meaning of that word, and the specific quality of moral goodness denoted by it. *Chrēstotēs* is goodness toward the evil and the ungrateful, it is beneficence towards enemies.

In the Sermon on the Mount, Jesus himself had already taught his disciples to see this as the distinctive quality of the kindness of God. We are to love our enemies and pray for our persecutors. 'Only so can you be children of your heavenly Father, who makes his sun rise on good and bad alike, and sends the rain on the honest and the dishonest' (Mt. 5:45 NEB). God is beneficent and kind to good and bad alike. He doesn't cause the sun to shine and the rain to fall on the crops of the good man, and withhold sun and rain from the crops of the bad man. 'He is kind to the ungrateful and the selfish' (Lk. 6:35).

The unmerited kindness of God has no limit. So the human kindness which comes from God must have no limits. 'If you love only those who love you, what reward can you expect? Surely the tax-gatherers do as much as that. And if you greet only your brothers, what is there extraordinary about that? Even the heathen do as much. There must be no limit to your goodness, as your heavenly Father's goodness knows no bounds' (Mt. 5:46-48 NEB). Something *extra*ordinary is required of the disciples of Christ, a kindness which goes beyond the common courtesies, beyond the limits of man's inclination and good nature. It's kindness with a plus in it.

These then, are the four characteristics of distinctive kindness. It comes from God in Christ; it lasts; it does not deal with others on the basis of their merits or deserts; it goes beyond the limits of man's inclination and good nature. We shall now look at these four characteristics in the people who 'have tasted the kindness of the Lord' (1 Pet. 2:3).

Four characteristics of kindness

The source of kindness is God. It is a transmitted quality. We first receive it from him and then pass it on to others.

> Have you had a kindness shown? Pass it on!
> 'Twas not given for thee alone. Pass it on!

These words of Henry Burton apply not only to human relationships but also to the divine-human relationship. He who has received kindness from God should pass it on to men. We cannot be kind to the Lord directly, but we can be kind to him indirectly. 'As you did it to one of the least of these my brethren, you did it to me' (Mt. 25:40). The motive is the imitation of Christ. Christians, all down the centuries, seeing in the gospels the kindness of Jesus, to children, to women, to lepers, to harlots and thieves, to Samaritans and Gentiles, to the sick in body and mind, to rich and poor, to tax-collectors and sinners, have deliberately set out to follow in his steps. We see his kindness, we express and embody his kindness in our personal relationships. It is the kindness which comes from the Lord and is passed on to men.

This kindness which comes from God abides. It lasts on; it doesn't end. That is not true of natural human kindness. It's easy to be kind to nice people in pleasant circumstances, but when the going is hard such kindness may disappear like mist before the rising sun. Fair-weather kindness may lead to disillusionment with human nature, unless we know the kindness which continues through all weathers. 'There are friends who pretend to be friends, but there is a friend who sticks closer than a brother' (Pr. 18:24). The kindness of Ruth to her widowed mother-in-law was not short-lived but permanent. To Naomi she declared her loyal love, her abiding kindness. 'Entreat me not to leave you or to return from following you; for where you go I will go, and where you lodge I will lodge; your people shall be my people, and your God my God; where you die I will die, and there will I be buried. May the Lord do so to me and more also if even death parts me from you' (Ru. 1:16-17). Ruth was determined that nothing, not even death, should part them. That is the type of Christian kindness. 'Love is kind...love never ends' (1 Cor. 13:4,8). It never disappears, never gives up; it doesn't fall down on its tasks.

This lasting kindness which has its source in God, has the plus, the extra in it. It goes the second mile. Eliezer asked Rebekah for a drink from her pitcher. She not only gave him a drink but she volunteered to water his camels as well. She did what she was asked and much more. That was kindness with the plus in it (Gn. 24:17-19). One characteristic of this extra is that it often goes beyond or even against our natural inclinations (Lk. 6:32-34). On the battlefield of Zutphen, Sir Philip Sidney, wounded and thirsty, was about to drink from his water-bottle. On seeing a dying soldier looking longingly at the bottle, he handed it over to him, saying, 'Thy need is yet greater than mine.' He overcame his strong natural inclination to satisfy his own thirst, in order to meet the greater need of another person. Many of those who minister to 'travellers', drop-outs, drug-addicts, alcoholics, or who work in geriatric wards, in mental hospitals, in prisons, may be offering a service which goes far beyond (and it may be against) their natural inclinations. That is kindness with the plus, the extra in it.

The distinctive quality of kindness

It was pointed out above that *chrēstotēs* has a distinctive meaning. It is kindness to those who don't deserve it, goodness to those who are evil, beneficence to those who are enemies. We see in some of the gospel stories, that this was distinctive of the kindness of Jesus. He associated with outcasts; he was 'a friend of tax-collectors and sinners' (Mt. 11:19). The tax-gatherers were ostracized by the righteous. Not only were they dishonest and rapacious; they were 'quislings', collecting taxes for the detested Romans, or their Jewish puppets. Jesus not only kept company with them, he also sat at the table with them. For the Jew, sharing food was a sign of intimate fellowship (Rev. 3:20). The Pharisees, the separated ones, were critical and hostile. 'This man receives sinners and eats with them' (Lk. 15:2). Jesus answered these criticisms by drawing attention to the need of the sinner and to the kindness of God. 'People who are well do not need a doctor, but only those who are sick. I have not come to call respectable people, but outcasts' (Mk. 2:17 GNB). God himself seeks the lost, and is overjoyed when they return to him (Lk. 15:1-10).

If we are kind like Jesus, shall we then keep company with people of doubtful morals? Here we have to walk on a knife-edge. 'Bad companions ruin good character', says Paul (1 Cor. 15:33 GNB). We have been warned! Children, some young people and adults lacking in maturity and stability of character, are well advised to 'shun evil companions'. He who touches tar gets black. On the other hand, he who keeps himself separate is not following in the master's steps. Those who are motivated by the kindness of Jesus, and share in his mission of seeking and saving the lost, will befriend people irrespective of their goodness or badness. The doctor must go to the patient, and take the risk of catching the disease.

In Christ, God is kind not only to the unworthy, but also to his enemies. 'We were God's enemies, but he made us his friends through the death of his Son' (Rom. 5:10 GNB). By kindness God turns his enemies into friends. If then we are to be like God, we too must love our enemies. We may seek to evade this challenge by saying that we have no enemies. In the sense of opponents we hate, fight and seek to destroy, that may well be true. So widen the meaning. Include the folk you dislike for one reason or another; the acquaintances whose idiosyncrasies and habits irritate and annoy you; the strangers of another colour or race who repel you just because they are different; the people whose political or religious views you detest. Understood in this inclusive sense, most of us have enemies of one kind or another. How can we love then?

In the chapter on *love*, it was pointed out that the command of Jesus, 'love your enemies' is followed by three imperatives which interpret it and show us how to obey it. 'Do good to those who hate you, bless those who curse you, pray for those who abuse you' (Lk. 6:27-28). Feelings cannot be commanded but actions can. If love were only a feeling or a sentiment it would not be possible for us to set out to love those we don't like. What we can do is to act in helpful ways towards those who repel us. Deliberately plan and carry out kind and helpful acts. Call down blessings and pray regularly for the people you dislike. It also helps immensely to get to know 'the enemy' as a person. Pet aversions and stubborn prejudices thrive on ignorance and hearsay. It's hard to dislike any person you know intimately. It's possible, but it's unusual. Perhaps the Pharisees, the separated ones, were critical of and hostile to bad men just because they did keep themselves separate. Through meeting and mixing, through involvement and identification with them, those who were our enemies can become our friends.

Transformation through kindness

Zacchaeus of Jericho was a wealthy man. Inspector of taxes in that important frontier city, he had ample opportunity to enrich himself by dishonesty and greed. As a result he was despised and ostracized; he was a social outcast. Zacchaeus was keen to see Jesus, but since he was a little man he was unable to do so because of the crowd. So he ran on ahead and climbed a sycamore tree to get a good view. When Jesus came to the tree, he looked up and called the tax-collector by name. 'Zacchaeus, make haste and come down; for I must stay at your house to-day' (Lk. 19:5). Descending in double-quick time, Zacchaeus received Jesus into his house joyfully. The respectable people were scandalized. 'He has gone in to be the guest of a man who is a sinner' (Lk. 19:7). But

Zacchaeus was impressed and transformed by the undeserved kindness of Jesus. In gratitude for the generosity of Jesus to him, and what Jesus had done for him, Zacchaeus decided to give half his goods to the poor and to restore four-fold whatever he had taken from others by extortion. He was converted by kindness; he was converted to kindness (Lk. 19:1-10).

Kindness has transforming power. It can bring about a complete change of outlook and direction in a person's life. The life of a French youth, fifteen years of age, was changed by a great and unexpected kindness. In winter, shivering with cold, he was tending a stall in the open-air market. A stranger, seeing his condition, went into a shop, bought a warm overcoat and a fur cap and gave them to him. This undeserved and unexpected kindness changed the lad's whole outlook. 'It made him see what he could do for other people. It started him out doing unexpected kindnesses to all sorts of strangers.'[7] For many of us learning a foreign language is a slow, difficult and painful business. Yet the commendable attempt to provide a universal language, *Esperanto*, has not met with success. For a language cannot be manufactured; it is a living thing, the product of the life, experience, history and culture of a people. There *is*, however, a universal language. Kindness is understood by all men everywhere. This is finely expressed by an anonymous author. 'Kindness is a language which the blind can see, and the deaf can hear.' Two missionaries to a primitive tribe in Papua found the problem of communication almost, but not quite, insuperable. This is their testimony. 'The natives do not understand our theology, but they understand our loving-kindness, and let themselves be won by it.'

The kindness of God has appeared in this world in Christ incarnate and crucified. That kindness which converts us can transform the lives of others through us. As kindness produces kindness, there is a crop of kindness in the field of the world. Then the word of the apostle Paul is fulfilled in another and different sense, 'the harvest of the Spirit is …kindliness' (Gal. 5:22 Moffatt).

Notes for chapter eight

1. From the poem, *Lines composed a few miles above Tintern Abbey.*
2. Adam Gordon, *Ye Wearie Wayfarer.*
3. *A Precocious Autobiography,* quoted from *The Fourth Lesson,* Book 1,
   C. Campling, ed. (Darton, Longman and Todd, 1973), pp.300-301.
4. William Barclay, *The Gospel of Mark* (St. Andrew Press, 1954), p.343.
5. L. H. Marshall, *The Challenge of New Testament Ethics* (Macmillan, 1946),
   pp.295-296.
6. *Ibid.,* p.296.
7. J. Reid, *Where the New World Begins* (Hodder and Stoughton, 1947), p.128.

9 Goodness

Goodness

'A man ran up and knelt before him, and asked him, "Good Teacher, what must I do to inherit eternal life?" And Jesus said to him, "Why do you call me good? No one is good but God alone"' (Mk. 10:17-18). God is 'the fountain of all goodness'.[1] Jesus directs the attention of the young ruler to God as the supreme and only good. That recognition comes before obedience. Prior to doing good, to keeping the commandments, is the acknowledgment that God is the one source of all goodness. There is a radical difference between the biblical conception of goodness and that of the humanist, whether ancient or modern. In the Bible, goodness is theocentric, not anthropocentric. It comes from God, not from man. God is like a perennial spring, and his goodness, like an ever-flowing stream, flows into the lives of those who are in right relationship with him.

This perfect goodness of the Father was revealed and embodied in the Son. The glory of God, his nature revealed, was seen in the face of Jesus Christ. Jesus pointed the young ruler away from himself to God, the source of all goodness, because the *human* goodness of Jesus came from God. He grew in goodness. 'Jesus increased in wisdom and in stature, and in favour with God and man' (Lk. 2:52). He 'learned obedience' and was made perfect through suffering (Heb. 5:8; 2:10). In the growth of his goodness there was no imperfection. Reading through the gospels, people in all ages have been impressed, as were the first disciples, by his complete goodness. The absence of defect and flaw rightly leads us to speak of his sinlessness. But 'sinlessness' is a negative term; what we find in Jesus is something intensely vital and positive, absolute goodness.

This perfect goodness of God, which is revealed in the character of Jesus, is made available to men through his work as Redeemer. 'By him we are put right with God; we become God's holy people and are set free' (1 Cor. 1:30 GNB). Through the redemption which is in Christ, the goodness of God is transferred to the believer by the Holy Spirit. As already pointed out, the adjective qualifying 'Spirit' is significant. The spirit who through Christ indwells believers is the *Holy* Spirit. The holy God, who is perfect goodness, requires his people to be holy; 'You shall be holy, for I am holy' (1 Pet. 1:16). It is in order that we may meet this requirement that he gives to us the Holy Spirit, who produces in us the goodness of Christ. And so it is from God, from the Holy Trinity, from the Father, the Son and the Holy Spirit, that all human goodness is derived. Goodness is gift, grace, fruit.

Being good and doing good

A distinction must be made between *being* good and *doing* good, between character and conduct. Jesus, we recall, speaks of a tree and of its fruit. In the ethical teaching of the Jewish legalists the emphasis was upon the fruit. What mattered was a man's words and deeds. As interpreted by the scribes it was with these that the law of Moses was primarily concerned. Evil words and deeds were prohibited; good words and deeds were commanded. In this respect scribal ethics were akin to those of the great philosopher. Aristotle taught that habit was the key to character. Men acquire a particular quality by constantly acting in a particular way. Make a habit of doing good and you will become good. Speak virtuous words and perform virtuous deeds, and in time you will become a virtuous person. As we shall observe below, there is an element of truth in this error. Good men do become better by habit; evil men do not. Motives are all-important. Any play-actor or opportunist can produce apparently good words and deeds to suit his purposes. A hypocrite can 'practise' piety (Mt. 6:1). The act appears to be good, but the motive is bad. A person who is selfish, dishonest, sensual, can masquerade behind virtuous words and deeds. For this reason, and for a time, it may be difficult to judge a person's character from his words and deeds. In the long term, however, the tree is known by its fruits. The hidden is revealed. The essential character, concealed by play-acting, comes to light (Lk: 12:2).

Jesus is concerned with the heart of man. For if the character is good then the conduct will take care of itself. 'Make the tree good, and its fruit good' (Mt. 12:33). How, then, is the tree to be made good? Jesus called men to repent and believe because the kingdom of God was at hand. He demanded a change of mind, a new disposition, a heart surrendered to the sovereignty of God. From this transformed outlook, this new heart, the fruit of good words and actions would issue spontaneously and inevitably. 'The good man out of his good treasure brings forth good, and the evil man out of his evil treasure brings forth evil' (Mt. 12:35). For Jesus, the good man is the man who enters the kingdom, the man who accepts the sovereignty of God and seeks to do the will of God. 'There is no Good save obedient behaviour, save the obedient will. But this obedience is rendered not to a law or principle which can be known beforehand, but only to the free, sovereign will of God. The Good consists in always doing what God wills at any particular moment. Human conduct can only be considered good when, and in so far as, God himself acts in it through the Holy Spirit.'[2]

Integrity and purity of heart

This teaching of Jesus on the nature of goodness was antici-pated in the Old Testament. 'Keep your heart with all vigilance; for from it flow the springs of life' (Pr. 4:23). Good conduct is a matter of the heart; that is, of the mind, the will and the emotions, of the inner man as a whole. If the heart is right with God good words and deeds flow from its hidden springs. When there is this consistency between what a man is within and what he is without, he is a man of integrity. That is authentic goodness; wholeness of heart. In the realm of numbers, *integer* is contrasted with *fraction*. Two-thirds, five-eighths, are fractions; something less than a whole number. An integer is a whole number, an undivided quantity, a thing complete. Integrity is the state of being complete, the component parts of the personality having been drawn together into one whole. Noah and Abraham were men of integrity (Gn. 6:9; 17:1). It is not sinlessness. It is, for example, attributed to David whose sinfulness is frankly recorded in Scripture. Yet he walked before God 'with integrity of heart and uprightness' (1 Ki. 9:4). David was not 'a double-minded man' (Jas. 1:7). He was whole-hearted in his devotion to the Lord.

This single-minded devotion to God is asked for and commended by Jesus. 'Blessed are the pure in heart, for they shall see God' (Mt. 5:8). True purity is not external but internal. It is secured not by washings and bathings of the body, but by the Holy Spirit who cleanses and unifies the heart. He answers the prayer of the psalmist, 'Unite my heart to fear thy name'; that is, make me single-minded (Ps. 86:11). The spirit fulfils the promise made to God's people, 'I will give them one heart and one way' (Je. 32:39). Pure means unmixed. Water is pure when it is free from any foreign substances. A metal is pure when it is without alloy. The pure man has been freed by the Spirit from duplicity, from mixed motives, from conflicting purposes. He is single-minded in his desire to do the will of God. Jesus called for this purity of motive in giving to the needy, in prayer and in fasting. The authentic man doesn't do the right thing with the wrong motive (Mt. 6:1-18). 'There is about the single-minded person an essential moral healthiness and a simple unaffected goodness, which are absent from those whose motives are more mixed and who are trying to serve more masters than one.'[3]

Doing good

We are now in a position to move on from *being* good to *doing* good. On one occasion Peter outlined the gospel to the Roman centurion Cornelius. He included a statement about the itinerant ministry and the good deeds of Jesus. 'He went about doing good' (Acts 10:38). Doing good was characteristic of Jesus; it had to be included among the few essentials of the gospel. In these days of swift and easy travel many of us go about far more than Jesus ever did. But do we go about doing good? Perhaps this confession of sin by Kagawa of Japan is more appropriate on our lips than on his:

> I read, in a book, that a man called Christ
> Went about doing good.
> It is very disconcerting to me,
>   that I am so easily satisfied
> With just – going about.

The emphasis placed by Jesus on goodness of heart does not mean that he devalued good deeds. It was because he *was* concerned about conduct, that he was concerned about character. 'Every sound tree bears good fruit…the good man out of his good treasure brings forth good' (Mt. 7:17; 12:35). From a good heart good deeds flow spontaneously. His eight-fold description of the character of the new man, the beatitudes, is climaxed by the command to do good. 'Your light must shine before people, so that they will see the good things you do and praise your Father in heaven' (Mt. 5:16 GNB). Profession without practice avails nothing (Mt. 7:21). The good deeds to which Jesus called his disciples are to be seen in his own ministry. He preached, he taught, he visited, he fed the hungry, he comforted the bereaved, he encouraged the despondent, he rescued those in danger, he helped the needy, he befriended the lonely, he healed the sick in body and in mind, he looked for, found and saved the lost, he gave service, he gave himself. The good deeds appropriate in his day are summed up in the parable of the Last Judgment. 'I was hungry and you gave me food, I was thirsty and you gave me drink, I was a stranger and you welcomed me, I was naked and you clothed me, I was sick and you visited me, I was in prison and you came to me' (Mt. 25:35-36).

With the teaching and example of Jesus before them, the apostles emphasized the importance of *doing* good. James, the brother of Jesus, insists on both faith and works. Without deeds, faith is not alive but dead. Good deeds are the evidence of true faith. 'I will show you my faith by my actions.' A mere profession of faith unproductive of good deeds is likened to a corpse (Jas. 2:18, 26 GNB). In his letters, especially to the Galatians and the Romans, the apostle Paul affirms that we are not saved by good deeds, but by grace through faith in Christ. He emphasizes, however, with James, that we are saved *for* good deeds. 'When we are in union with Christ Jesus...what matters is faith that works through love' (Gal. 5:6 GNB). Doing good isn't an optional extra, it is God's original purpose for Christians. 'God has made us what we are, and in our union with Christ Jesus he has created us for a life of good deeds, which he has already prepared for us to do' (Eph. 2:10 GNB). If we live as God wills, our 'lives will produce all kinds of good deeds', and we shall never 'become tired of doing good' (Col. 1:10; Gal. 6:9 GNB). In those parts of his letters concerned with conduct (*e.g.* Romans, chapters 12 and 13) Paul gives many examples of what it means to do good. Such concrete instances do not exhaust the possibilities for us today. For 'the appearances of good are as numerous as the faces of our neighbours. There can be no question of asking the Scriptures for a complete description of good.'[4] The Holy Spirit will show us in our circumstances what we are to do today. But the two spheres for doing good are still the same, in the world and in the church. 'As often as we have the chance, we should do good to everyone, and especially to those who belong to our family in the faith' (Gal. 6:10 GNB). So then, according to the New Testament, goodness is not only a quality of character, it is also an activity. It has legs and arms: it goes and does. He who is good, does good. The biography of a Christian, like that of the Master, should be, he (she) 'went about doing good'.

Goodness and purpose

The goodness which is the fruit of the Spirit must be seen not only in terms of character and activity, of being good and doing good: it must also be understood in terms of purpose and vocation. A Christian is certainly not called to be 'good for nothing'. True goodness has a function, an activity proper to itself by which it fulfils its purpose. The two little words *at* and *for* best describe this aspect of goodness. In common speech we refer to a person as being good *at* something. John is good at figures, Peter is good at farming, David is good at administration. Joan is good at typing, Mary at gardening, Margaret at cooking. Mr Carter is a good pilot, Mrs Smith is a good doctor, Mr Brown is a good bus-driver. These expressions refer to the functions of the people cited, to the effective discharge of the activities proper to their calling.

This meaning is inherent in the affirmation of Jesus, 'I am the good shepherd' (Jn. 10:11). There is an implied contrast with the bad shepherds of Israel, described and condemned by the prophet Ezekiel (Ezk. 34:1-10). The shepherds or rulers of Israel had not fed the sheep, healed the sick, bound up the crippled, brought back the strayed, protected the flock from wild beasts. They had failed to carry out the responsibilities of their calling. In contrast to those worthless shepherds, Jesus is the good shepherd. He feeds, he guides, he protects his sheep. He knows them individually, intimately, and lays down his life on their behalf. Jesus is good *at* shepherding. Now since it is the goodness of Jesus that the Spirit produces in believers, they too will be good *at* — whatever it is that God has called and endowed them to do. To be good is to be useful. 'Each one, as a good manager of God's different gifts, must use for the good of others the special gift he has received from God' (1 Pet. 4:10 GNB).

For is an even better word than *at* to describe this particular characteristic of goodness. In my hand is a pen. It's a good pen. It isn't a virtuous or ethical pen! In calling it a good pen, I mean that it is good *for* writing. A good car runs well; it is good *for* transport. The phrase 'a good horse' could refer to a race-horse, to a pony or to a cart-horse. The first is good for speed and sport, the second for the children to ride, the third for work on the farm. Function and activity, usefulness and purpose, are an essential part of the meaning of the word *good* when used in these contexts. This is true supremely of the goodness attributed to Jesus Christ. As we saw when outlining his character in chapter two, his goodness is inseparable from his vocation. It is goodness *for*, goodness with a goal. His life on earth, as portrayed in the gospels, was dominated by a purpose. He didn't drift down the stream of time; he had a clear vision, a single aim, a steadfast purpose. He lived for the kingdom, he lived for God. His goodness and his dedication to his vocation are as inseparable as the two sides of a coin.

If we live in accordance with the character and example of Jesus Christ by the power of the Holy Spirit, then our lives also will have the *for* in them, will be dominated by a purpose. This is clearly seen in the life of Paul who wrote about goodness as a fruit of the Spirit. He could say, 'For me to live is Christ, and to die is gain' (Phil. 1:21). Paul's life was fully dedicated to the service of Christ, to the ceaseless attempt to make him known to others. A good Christian is a person who lives for Christ. This does not mean that a committed Christian has a one-track mind or a solitary interest. Many tributaries flow into the Rhine as it wends its way from the Swiss Alps to the North Sea; but they all contribute to the one stream. A Christian should have a wide and varied range of interests, but they should all be tributaries feeding the mainstream of life. They should all contribute to the one *for*, the dominant purpose. The Christian soldier, says Paul, does not get entangled in a variety of conflicting purposes, 'since his aim is to satisfy the one who enlisted him' (2 Tim. 2:4). Why did Christ die for us and rise again? 'He died for all, that those who live might live no longer for themselves but for him who for their sake died and was raised' (2 Cor. 5:15). Note the stark contrast; men who live *for* themselves, men who live *for* Christ. A good woman or man is a person who lives for Christ.

Goodness as generosity

Goodness is a general term with a wide range of meaning. For this reason, this sixth fruit of the Spirit, *agathōsynē*, is difficult to define exactly. In particular, how does goodness differ from kindness, the virtue which precedes it in Paul's list? Dr J. B. Lightfoot suggests that the word *kindness* refers to a kindly disposition, whereas goodness is kindness in action, kindness taking a practical form.[5] This distinction, however, does not hold, for the New Testament knows nothing of an inactive kindness. There is a better way to understand the distinctive meaning of goodness. Those words which begin with the syllable *bene* best describe the good man: He is benevolent and beneficent; he is a benefactor, the bestower of many benefits. In a word, goodness is generosity.

Goodness as generosity is the theme of a parable of Jesus. A householder went out early in the morning and hired labourers for his vineyard. The rate was a silver coin a day. He went out again at the third, sixth, ninth and eleventh hours to engage additional labourers. When evening came, all the workers, irrespective of the number of hours they had worked, were paid one silver coin, the full day's wage. When those who had been hired at dawn complained because those who had worked fewer hours received as much as they, the employer replied with a question. 'Is thine eye evil (*poneros* = mean) because I am good?' The Revised Standard Version translates it, 'Do you begrudge my generosity?' (Mt. 20:15 AV and RSV). The householder is said to be good because he is generous, for to pay a day's wage for half a day's work, even for as little as one hour, is generous indeed! That is how God in Christ deals with us. Those to whom God is good should themselves be generous to others. Because we 'know how generous our Lord Jesus Christ has been', we are urged in turn to be open-handed and open-hearted in all our dealings with others (2 Cor. 8:9 NEB).

This distinctive quality of Christian goodness is to be seen in the character and conduct of one of the apostles. Barnabas is described as 'a good man' (Acts 11:24). At a time when many Christians were sharing their goods, Luke introduces him in his narrative as a typical example of generosity. 'Thus Joseph who was surnamed by the apostles Barnabas (which means, Son of encouragement), a Levite, a native of Cyprus, sold a field which belonged to him, and brought the money and laid it at the apostles' feet.' 'Son of encouragement' is a

Hebrew idiom, a way of saying that the outstanding characteristic of Barnabas was the encouragement he gave to others. When the Christians would have nothing to do with the newly-converted Saul of Tarsus, it was Barnabas who believed in him and introduced him to the church in Jerusalem. From that same church, Barnabas was sent out to encourage the converts at Antioch 'to remain faithful to the Lord' (Acts 4:36-37; 9:27; 11:22-23). 'Barnabas indeed is one of the most attractive characters in the New Testament. He possessed the rare gift of discerning merit in others. Probably inferior in ability to Paul, he was his superior in Christian graces. He seems to have been utterly without jealousy, eager to excuse the faults of others, quick to recognize merit, ready to compromise for the sake of peace.'[6] Goodness, as seen in Barnabas, is generosity of hand, of mind and of heart.

The beauty of holiness

Goodness, generosity – and beauty. The Hebrew word for good (*tob*) is used not only of the ethically and morally good but also of that which is attractive, pleasant and beautiful. We find this word at the very beginning of the Bible. 'God saw everything that he had made, and behold, it was very good' (Gn. 1:31). All that God brings into existence is perfect, harmonious and beautiful. The good is also that which is pleasant and attractive to the senses. Good wine, good figs, good honey, are agreeable to the sense of taste. The good-looking girl, Rebekah, and the healthy baby, the 'goodly child' Moses, are a delight to the eyes. In the Greek Bible the two words for good, *agathos* and *kalos*, are practically synonymous. In some contexts, however, *kalos* is used, not in the sense of morally good but rather of that which is pleasant and beautiful. Thus God led the Hebrews out of Egypt to 'a good and broad land' (Ex. 3:8). As used here of the Promised Land, *good* means fertile and fruitful, pleasant and beautiful.

When the character or the conduct of a person is said to be *good*, both the moral and the aesthetic meanings may be combined. Recall, for example, the deed in which Mary of Bethany expressed her love for Jesus. That was an act of extravagant generosity. The answer of Jesus to the criticism of those present was, 'She has done a beautiful thing to me' (Mt. 26:10). Mary's act of generosity was not only morally good; it was also fitting and appropriate, attractive and lovely. The word *kalos* may be used not only of an action but also of a person. The Lord Jesus Christ is described as 'the good shepherd'. 'The shepherd, the beautiful one – of course this translation exaggerates. But it is important that the word for *good* here is one that represents, not the moral rectitude of goodness nor its austerity, but its attractiveness.'[7]

It is this final ingredient, beauty, grace, which makes genuine Christian goodness attractive. It's of vital importance that it should be attractive, for it's difficult, if not impossible, to be 'enthusiastic for good' (1 Pet. 3:13 J. B. Phillips), if the good people we know don't appeal to us. Goodness has been devalued for some because they have been repelled by the so-called good people they have had the misfortune to know. Recall Paul's distinction between a righteous man and a good man. We can respect the strictly upright, but we aren't drawn to them. For some, the word *good* has been contaminated by its association with *goody-goody*, or with the *do-gooder*, or with a *holier-than-thou* attitude to others. All such might well be tempted to pray the prayer of a mother superior. 'Keep me reasonably sweet; I do not want to be a saint – some of them are so hard to live with!'

It was said of Sir Philip Sidney that he had 'a sweet attractive kind of grace'. The true saints, whether or not they have *St* before their names, make goodness attractive. They help us to overcome evil with good, by making the good more attractive than the evil. They are like Orpheus rather than Ulysses in the old Greek story. Wicked sirens who lived on an island in the sea often lured sailors to death on the rocks by their bewitching songs. Ulysses escaped disaster by stopping up the ears of his mariners with wax; deaf to the sirens' song, they rowed on past the island to safety. Orpheus had a better plan. He was a superb musician. As his ship approached the dangerous island he played his lute. The music of Orpheus was more attractive to the crew than the songs of the sirens. The sailors rowed on to safety, enraptured. Christ is the

157

Orpheus who triumphs over evil not by exclusion ('see no evil, hear no evil') but by making goodness more attractive.

The Scottish Christian, Henry Drummond, himself a fine example of the magnetism of goodness, wrote of the marvellous grace and beauty to be seen in the ministry of Jesus. 'Look at the exquisite loveliness, beauty and grace which characterized all the actions of Jesus. There is a marvellous grace about each and all; there is an attractive peculiarity which calls forth unbidden our deepest love and admiration. What is it? It is the Beauty of Holiness.' What is most attractive about Jesus, however, is his supreme act of generosity and grace, his sacrifice and death on the cross. As a magnet draws iron filings to itself, so Christ crucified has drawn to himself people from all races and centuries. 'I, when I am lifted up from the earth, will draw all men to myself' (Jn. 12:32). We too can be drawn by the magnet of his wonderful love and feel the pull of his Spirit, the Holy Spirit, when we fix our eyes on Jesus and see in him the beauty of holiness.

Notes for chapter nine

1. *Book of Common Prayer*, Prayer for the Royal Family.
2. Emil Brunner, *The Divine Imperative* (Lutterworth, 1937), pp.83-84.
3. R. V. G. Tasker, *Matthew* (Tyndale New Testament Commentaries, IVP, 1961), p.76.
4. R. Neil, article on Good, *Vocabulary of the Bible*, J. J. Allmen, ed. (Lutterworth, 1958), p.154.
5. J. B. Lightfoot, *Galatians* (Macmillan, 1865), p.213.
6. F. J. Foakes Jackson, *The Acts of the Apostles* (Hodder and Stoughton, 1931), p.100.
7. William Temple, *Readings in St. John's Gospel* (Macmillan, 1947), p.166.

10 Faithfulness

One word: three meanings

During the weekly radio programme, Desert Island Discs, Roy Plomley always asks his guest this question, 'The Bible and Shakespeare excepted, what book would you choose to have with you on the desert island?' A good case could be made for *The Oxford English Dictionary*, for words can be an inexhaustible source of interest. One of the fascinating things about them is that they can have multiple meanings. A word has not necessarily a uniform and invariable connotation. Its meaning may depend upon its setting in history and culture, or upon the context in which it is used in speech or writing. These considerations apply especially to the Greek word *pistis*, used to designate the seventh of the fruits of the Spirit. This word is translated into English as *faith* in the Authorized Version, *faithfulness* in the Revised Standard Version and the Good News Bible, *fidelity* in the New English Bible and as *trustfulness* in the Jerusalem Bible. As used by Paul, the word *pistis* has three meanings.

1. *Faith is trust.* God sends preachers of the word, and faith depends on and is called forth by the gospel proclaimed. It is 'hearing with faith' the message of salvation, the good news of deliverance through Christ crucified and risen. To have faith is to trust and to entrust our lives to God who encounters us in Christ as Saviour and Lord. It is total response and total acceptance, the response of the whole person, the mind, the will and the emotions, to all that God has done for us and

offers to us in Christ. This is the faith that justifies, that sets us in right relationship with God, and makes us acceptable to him through Jesus Christ (Gal. 3:2; Rom. 5:1-2; 10:14-15).

2. *Faith is a special endowment for service.* As such, it is not like justifying faith common to all Christians. It is a gift, a *charisma*, entrusted to some and not to others. Paul uses the word *pistis* to designate the third of the nine *gifts* of the Spirit (1 Cor. 12:9). It is an endowment for a special task. Borrowing a rich picture from Jesus, Paul writes of the faith that removes mountains (Mk. 11:23; 1 Cor. 13:2). Picture language should not always be taken literally. Faith doesn't move mountains of earth, but it can triumph over apparently insuperable obstacles. The minutest quantity of this kind of faith can achieve things which to men seem impossible (Mt. 17:20). Jesus associated faith of this kind with prayer. It is the firm conviction that God will answer our prayers and take action to meet our needs in a specific situation. To give two examples, one from Scripture and one from church history: it is the faith of the prophet Elijah on Mount Carmel calling down fire from heaven; it is the faith of George Müller of Bristol, praying for voluntary contributions for the maintenance of some two thousand orphans.

3. *Faith is faithfulness.* It is a quality of character. When the word is used of God himself it has reference to his firmness and reliability, his steadfastness and faithfulness. It is with this meaning that Paul uses *pistis* to describe the seventh fruit of the Spirit. The Holy Spirit creates and produces in the believer constancy, faithfulness. The spiritual man is loyal, reliable, dependable. There is, of course, an inseparable connection between faith in the first and in the third definitions of the word; between faith as a theological and faith as an ethical virtue. For he who has faith in the faithful God, himself becomes faithful. The believer becomes like the Lord in whom he trusts. The fruit of genuine faith is fidelity. The man of faith becomes the faithful man; the people of faith become 'the faithful'. 'To have faith is the seed and root of religion: to keep faith is the flower and fruit of religion.'[1]

The Rock: the faithfulness of God

I was born and brought up in a tiny village in the heart of rural Cheshire. Opposite my home is a hill rising 365 feet from the surrounding plain, Beeston Castle. The hill is surmounted by the Rock, a lofty, jagged crag, the nesting place of crows, falling sheer 200 feet to the hillside. As a boy, I often climbed up to the Rock and sat looking out over the fertile Cheshire Plain to the mountains of North Wales. Returning to those scenes of childhood after half a century, I find that many things have changed or disappeared. Methods of farming have changed beyond recognition, and almost all the people I once knew have gone. The Rock, however, remains unchanged. True, a meticulous person could point out that even the hard sandstone rock is subject to gradual erosion. Granted, but over against man and his activities, the Rock is a symbol of the unchanging, the permanent.

In several places in the Old Testament the phrase *the Rock* is used as a grand title for God. Derived from the natural scenery of the central highlands of Palestine, the Rock is a figure for the constancy of God. 'The Rock, his work is perfect; for all his ways are justice. A God of faithfulness and without iniquity, just and right is he' (Dt. 32:4). Like a crag, God is unchangeable, reliable, eternally dependable. This faithfulness of God is revealed in the order and constancy of nature. 'While the earth remains, seedtime and harvest, cold and heat, summer and winter, day and night, shall not cease' (Gn. 8:22). The rhythms and sequences, and what are today called 'the laws of nature', these are the habits of God, his customary procedures, exhibiting his faithfulness to all creation. We can rely on them because we can rely on him. This 'covenant of preservation' is with a view to the 'covenant of grace'. 'The natural orders, fixed by God's word, mysteriously guarantee a world in which in his own time God's historical saving activity will begin.'[2] The Creator is the Lord of the covenant who is faithful to the promises made to Israel through Abraham, Moses and David. To those who keep his covenant and obey his commandments, the loyal love of the Lord is from everlasting to everlasting (Ps. 103:17-18)

God's unvarying attitude towards Israel, his faithfulness to his covenant and promises, is the one and only ground of his people's faithfulness. It is God alone who makes the believer firm and trustworthy. This truth is taught negatively by Isaiah and positively by Habakkuk. King Ahaz refused to trust in God, to rely upon the covenant made by God with his ancestor David, promising the permanence of the Davidic dynasty (2 Sa. 7:16). To the faithless king, Isaiah says, 'If you will not believe, surely you shall not be established' (Is. 7:9). In the Hebrew there is a play upon words. 'If your faith is not firm and sure (*tha' aminn*) then you will not be established and secure' (*the' amenn*). A century and a half later, when Judah was threatened by another foe, the prophet Habakkuk was agonizing over the problem of evil. Why were the cruel and arrogant Chaldeans allowed to conquer the Judeans, who for all their faults were more righteous than the oppressor? To the faithful Judeans the prophet declares, 'The righteous shall live by his faithfulness' (Hab. 2:4 margin). The Holy One, the Rock, is absolutely sure, completely trustworthy. He is faithful. Against all appearances to the contrary, the people of God must hold on to his word without wavering. Trusting thus in the trustworthy God, they themselves will be made firm and reliable. They will not necessarily be able to read the meaning of events, to understand intellectually the problems by which they are confronted. But in such circumstances, and at all times, they will live by fidelity, steadfastness, faithfulness.

Christ: faithful and true

The faithfulness of God is fully disclosed in the life and character, the ministry and the passion of Jesus Christ. As we saw in chapter two, fidelity is a virtue of the vocation of Jesus, who was utterly loyal to the will and purpose of his Father. His faithfulness can be seen and understood only in terms of loyalty to a cause, of dedication to a task, of commitment to a mission. As a boy of twelve he was already dedicated to his Father's business, and throughout his life and ministry his dominant desire was to do the will and work of God. 'My food is to obey the will of the one who sent me and to finish the work he gave me to do' (Jn. 4:34 GNB). 'Like the Mississippi through the centre of the continent, gathering the contribution of the brooks and rivers on every side, this central dedication of the Master flowed down through his life and everything was made to pay tribute to it.'[3]

This fidelity of Jesus is to be seen most clearly and fully in the light of the goal of his vocation. The ministry is the preface to the passion. 'He set his face to go to Jerusalem' (Lk. 9:51). He knew what would befall him there; yet neither enemy nor friend could turn him from the way to the cross. With resolute constancy he moved on to his destiny. In Gethsemane, overwhelmed with horror and dismay, his heart breaking with grief, he surrendered to the will of God. He did not falter next day before the Roman governor, but remained steadfast in word and deed. He 'firmly professed his faith before Pontius Pilate' (1 Tim. 6:13 GNB). He was faithful unto death.

On the Isle of Patmos, John received his revelation 'from Jesus Christ the faithful witness, the first-born of the dead, and the ruler of kings on earth' (Rev. 1:5). Here *the faithful witness* means the faithful martyr. Jesus bore witness to God's way of overcoming evil, the way of the cross, and was vindicated by God who raised him from the dead and exalted him above all rule and authority. This exalted and reigning Lord is our great high priest and mediator, who ever lives to make intercession for us. What he was on earth, faithful, fitted him for what he is in heaven, faithful. He qualified for his ministry in the school of suffering here below, where he never faltered or swerved in his vocation. He is now and for ever in heaven, 'a merciful and faithful high priest' (Heb. 2:17). Moses, as leader, was faithful as a servant of the people of God: Jesus is faithful as Son over the household of God (Heb. 3:2). When he comes forth from that heaven at the end of the age, he will be revealed to all as 'Faithful and True' (Rev. 19:11). Trustworthy as the suffering Messiah on earth, he will come again in glory as the trustworthy and authentic Messiah from heaven. His name, his nature revealed, is *faithful*.

Constancy in prayer and worship

We turn now to faithfulness in the character and conduct of the Christian, and take up the two main truths already emphasized. He who trusts in the faithful God becomes faithful, and this faithfulness of the Christian, like that of Christ, has to do with his vocation. Now the calling or vocation of a Christian has two aspects. These may be variously described as the inner and the outer, contemplation and action, prayer and practice, worship and service. They are exemplified in the two sisters of Bethany. While Mary sat at the feet of Jesus and listened to his words, Martha was preoccupied with all the work she had to do (Lk. 10:38-42). We begin with the more important of the two aspects, the better part, that chosen by Mary, fellowship with the Lord.

Here is a typical question put to a candidate for baptism, confirmation and church membership. 'Do you, as a member of the Christian Church, promise to make use of the means of grace by being faithful in Bible reading and prayer, and joining regularly in public worship and in the sacrament of the Lord's Supper?'[4] This question arises from the conviction that continuance in the Christian life depends upon faithfulness in devotion, personal and communal. It does. No-one, in fact, who forgets all about him, or who rarely if ever thinks about him, speaks to him, listens to his word, receives his gifts, can be faithful to the Lord. So the candidate for baptism promises to be faithful in his use of the four, two personal, two corporate, means of grace, Bible reading and prayer, church worship and sacrament.

In all four, faithfulness means regularity. Both Christ and his apostles stress the need for constancy in prayer (Lk. 11:5-10; 18:1; Acts 1:14; 2:42; Rom. 12:12; Col. 4:2; 1 Thes. 5:17). Because of the inconstancy of our nature it is helpful to have a rule for the devotional life, such as the following, 'Unless unavoidably prevented, I will read the Bible and pray every day, and I will join in public worship and receive the sacrament every week.' Many Christians would want to improve on that modest guide-line. It's an excellent thing to set aside *two* periods every day for communion with the Lord.

For obviously it is fitting to begin and to end each day with God. Rise in good time, wash and dress, and then before breakfast keep the morning watch with God. At the other end of the day there is usually more time available for Bible reading, meditation and prayer. Some Christians read and pray just before or after the evening meal, while they are still fresh and alert; others do so on retiring to the bedroom for the night. What is good for one may not be for another.

Not only in private prayer but also in congregational worship, constancy is necessary. 'Let us not give up the habit of meeting together' (Heb. 10:25 GNB). The early Christians met habitually to do four things. 'They met constantly to hear the apostles teach, and to share the common life, to break bread, and to pray' (Acts 2:42 NEB). It is an excellent habit to meet once or twice every Lord's Day with God's people, to hear his word read and preached, and to offer up together the spiritual sacrifices of praise and prayer. And happy is the Christian who every Sunday, or at least once or twice a month, joins in the celebration of the death and resurrection of Jesus Christ, entering into communion with the living and present Lord in the sacrament of his body and blood. In this busy and hectic age we are not likely to *find* time for the Lord, daily and weekly; we have to *make* it, to set it aside. A rule can help those who are tempted to be slack and negligent in the struggle against laziness and inertia. For the house of prayer and worship cannot be built on the shifting sands of feeling and mood; it *can* be built on the firm rock of disciplined habit and steadfast will. So we have to make time, lest, like Martha, we become 'distracted with much serving' and 'anxious and troubled about many things', and have no time to sit at the feet of Jesus and listen to his words.

From little things to great

To praise Mary is not to disparage Martha. Communion is better than service, but the latter is also an essential and should be an inseparable part of the Christian vocation. Look again at our example. Jesus was a man of prayer and a man of action; to follow him is to be faithful in both. Teresa of

Avila, Spanish mystic and reformer, combined contemplation and prayer with boundless activity and practical achievement. In her classic *The Interior Castle* she writes, 'Believe me, Martha and Mary must go together in entertaining our Lord.' So we turn from prayer to practice. We shall look now at faithfulness in various spheres: in the use of money, in daily work and voluntary service, in friendship and marriage, and finally in persecution and martyrdom.

If we are to be faithful in the practical affairs of life then we must recognize the importance of little things. Jesus once quoted a popular proverb. 'He who is faithful in a very little is faithful also in much; and he who is dishonest in a very little is dishonest also in much.' For most of us, most of the time, life is made up of small things. We rarely have the opportunity of doing great things. So, if we wait for the big occasions to practise fidelity we shall never get started. Small services, humdrum tasks, at home and at work, in the church and in the world, can be done with faithfulness. No doubt Jesus made excellent yokes and ploughs in the carpenter's workshop long before he became a faithful preacher, physician and Saviour. This principle – from faithfulness in little things to faithfulness in great things – Jesus applied to the use of money. He made a two-fold comparison between money and the true riches of God's kingdom. The one is of little value in comparison with the other; the money doesn't belong to us, but the true riches do. Money belongs to God and is entrusted to us; God's gifts, the true riches, are our own, and for keeps. Jesus issued a warning in the form of a question. 'If you have not been faithful in that which another's (money), who will give you that which is your own?' The converse of that grim warning is a splendid promise. If we are faithful in the use of money, God will give us his abundant wealth, and we can keep it for ever (Lk. 16:10-12).

Fidelity has to do with money, with our pockets and purses, our wages and salaries. As an entrustment from God money is to be used responsibly in all spheres of life. That responsibility to God must include what we spend on ourselves and our families, what we invest and how and what we give away. We should certainly give to those who are in need, to the work of our local church and to the mission of the church in the world. Paul has in mind the first of these, philanthropy, when he lays down the guidelines for Christian giving. What he says about that can also be applied to the support of the local church and to missionary work and outreach. 'Every Sunday each of you is to put aside and keep by him a sum in proportion to his gains' (1 Cor. 16:2 NEB). Giving should be regular. It should not be dependent on passing whim or impulse. We are to give weekly, 'every Sunday'. Giving should be proportionate. The general principle is, the more I earn, the more I should give. Since income and commitments are liable to frequent changes nowadays, the faithful Christian will work out carefully from time to time the total weekly sum to be given. Giving should be out of gratitude. Elsewhere, the apostle refers to the motive. 'For you know how generous our Lord Jesus Christ has been' (2 Cor. 8:9 NEB). We are to keep his self-emptying and sacrifice before our eyes, and out of sheer gratitude let our giving be a response to his.

Daily work and voluntary service

We are called to be faithful not only in the way we use our money but also in the way we do our work. There are not two kinds of work, sacred and secular, church work and daily work, Christian service and our jobs. The faithful Christian will seek to serve God in all his activities, and to transform each task into divine service. We can, however, make a valid distinction between the work for which we are paid and the work for which we are not paid. In both these spheres alike, in daily work and in voluntary service, we should do all things with the intention of pleasing God. 'Whatever your task, work heartily, as serving the Lord and not men' (Col. 3:23).

I am often asked to supply a reference or testimonial for a person applying for a job. On the form to be returned, worded in various ways, is the same leading question, 'Is the applicant honest and trustworthy, dependable and reliable?' Three qualities of character are implicit in this basic require-ment: regularity, honesty, diligence. A good employee is not an absentee. Unless unavoidably prevented, the worker can be relied on to turn up for work at the appointed times. At work, the faithful worker is honest, straight, upright, in all matters relating to money and property. That's not an easy virtue in an age when shoplifting has assumed epidemic proportions, when 'borrowing' things from the firm is wide-spread and when concocting phoney expense accounts is a common practice. A good worker is also conscientious. He or she gets on with the job and gives a good day's work for a good day's pay.

None of these qualities — regularity, honesty, diligence – is exciting or spectacular. Nor is another similar character-istic of fidelity in the worker, the ability to plod. Some of the jobs we have to do are dull and dreary. In this industrial age work is often monotonous, a constant repetition of the same actions. Voluntary service isn't usually as bad as that, but it isn't always interesting and rewarding. There are times 'when our burdens seem too heavy, life is dull and monoto-nous, and the hard road stretches endlessly before us'. Almost every servant of Christ, at one time or another, has to contend with dark moods and spiritual dryness, with frustrations and delays, with disappointments and apparent lack of results. At such times fidelity is to keep on, to plod.

Friendship and marriage

Faithfulness has to do not only with tasks but also with relationships, not only with work but also with people. It is a virtue of life in community. Jesus gave it priority. He criti-cized the scribes and Pharisees for their lack of a sense of proportion. Meticulous in tithing minute amounts of mint, dill and cummin, herbs of the kitchen garden, they were neglecting 'the weightier demands of the Law, justice, mercy, and good faith' (*pistis*) (Mt. 23:23 NEB). Here, fidelity has reference to the spoken word. The religious leaders were in the habit of going back on their pledged word, of making promises they did not keep. God loves the man whose words can be relied on, who does what he says he will do, who honours his verbal commitments. In business affairs his word is his bond. He stands by a deal even if he is the loser. He is not a gazumper! What he says can be relied on; what he undertakes he carries through. When good faith is in men's hearts and on their lips, then social life rests on a secure foundation.

Of the many ingredients which go into the making and keeping of friends, fidelity is of prime importance. For there are friends and friends! There is the fair-weather friend who disappears in a time of adversity, and there is a friend who 'loves at all times' and 'sticks closer than a brother' (Pr. 14:20; 17:17; 18:24; 19:4, 6-7). In the Apocrypha, Ben-Sira sings the praises of the constant friend. A Hebrew, he expresses the superlative by repeating the key word three times.

A faithful friend is a sure shelter,
    whoever finds one has found a rare treasure.
A faithful friend is something beyond price,
    there is no measuring his worth.
A faithful friend is the elixir of life,
    and those who fear the Lord will find one
                    (Ecclus. 6:14-16 JB)

A loyal friend is an unfailing source of strength and security. He enriches life beyond all telling and is a sovereign remedy for all our ills. So we do well to take Shakespeare's advice concerning those who have stuck with us over the years.

The friends thou hast, and their adoption tried,
Grapple them to thy soul with hoops of steel.

Marriage, according to Jeremy Taylor, is 'the queen of friendships', and the essential basis of true marriage is permanence. As portrayed in an Old Testament allegory, marriage is founded on loyal love. Gomer, wife of the prophet Hosea, was unfaithful to her husband. Having given birth to two children of which he was not the father, she left him and became a temple prostitute. Hosea continued to love his faithless wife, and eventually he rescued her from the slavery into which she had drifted. First he brought her back into his home and then later restored the marital relationship. In the light of his own tragic experience, he came to understand the nature of the relationship between Israel and her Lord. This is the conviction which underlies Hosea's allegory, 'If I, an imperfect and sinful human being, love my wife so much, and, in spite of her infidelity, cannot cease to love her, then how much more must the Lord love his faithless people Israel.' The faithful God would not give up his faithless people. After Israel had been disciplined in exile, God would restore her. 'I will betroth you to me in faithfulness; and you shall know the Lord' (Ho. 2:20). Whatever we do, God is faithful. 'If we are faithless, he remains faithful – for he cannot deny himself' (2 Tim. 2:13 and see Rom. 3:3). This fidelity of God should be the model, inspiration and basis of the relationship of husband and wife. Marriage is a covenant; and loyal-love, faithful love, is the joy and the obligation of those who have entered into and made the covenant. 'I, John Thomas, do take you, Mary Jane, to be my lawful wedded wife…for better for worse…to love and to cherish, till death us do part, and to this I pledge myself.' While faithfulness has a negative aspect, not having sexual relationships outside marriage – it is essentially a positive affirmation of and commitment to the marriage partner. The inner desires of the heart as well as the outward acts of conduct are involved. It is to love and to cherish at all times and in all circumstances, seeking the highest welfare of the partner within a commitment which is total and permanent. At a time when divorce is on the increase, the distinctive faithfulness which the Holy Spirit produces and maintains should be exhibited to the world…in Christian marriage and the Christian family.

Heroic faithfulness

The faithfulness of Jesus Christ, as we have already seen, was heroic. He didn't only plod on; he was opposed and persecuted, he was tempted and tried, he was condemned and crucified. He was faithful unto death. It's this quality of the character of Christ, fidelity of this calibre, that the Holy Spirit creates in a Christian. For there are times in life when we too have to swim against the stream, against a strong current of trials and temptations, of opposition and persecution. At such times plodding faithfulness is supplemented; the Spirit endows the believer with the heroic faithfulness of Christ.

During the first century, Christians were subject to opposition and persecution, direct or indirect, petty or severe, at the hands of their Jewish or pagan neighbours. Some Christians were threatened with a fiery ordeal (1 Pet. 4:12). Persecution instigated by Jew or Roman could be such that believers were confronted with death. Some were prepared to face even that prospect without wavering. It's in that context that the word *faithful* is used in the Apocalypse of John. The Christians at Pergamum, for example, did not flinch or draw back when persecuted and threatened with martyrdom. This despite the fact that one of their number, Antipas, had already been put to death. The Risen Lord calls Antipas 'my witness, my faithful one'. Here the Greek word *martys* means both witness and martyr. Antipas, who has borne witness by his death, receives the title *faithful*, the title of Jesus Christ himself (Rev. 2:13; 3:14).

The Christians at nearby Smyrna, soon to be persecuted, and in some cases imprisoned, are encouraged with this message, 'Do not fear what you are about to suffer. Behold, the devil is about to throw some of you into prison, that you may be tested, and for ten days you will have tribulation. Be faithful unto death, and I will give you the crown of life' (Rev. 2:10). Satan, working through the Roman authorities, would, for a short time, persecute and imprison some of the believers. The Risen Lord requires those who are faced with death to follow his own example. If death is to be the price of loyalty, then let them 'be faithful unto death'. The demand is coupled with a promise. A victor in the games received a fading crown of laurels; the victorious martyr will receive the unfading crown of immortality.

These examples of heroic faithfulness from Pergamum and Smyrna are from the distant past. But the persecution of Christians is by no means a thing of the past. In many parts of the world today, Christians are being harassed and persecuted directly, and more often indirectly. Many have been imprisoned and put to death in this twentieth century for their loyalty to Christ. So in your prayers, 'remember those in prison as if you were there with them; and those who are being maltreated, for you like them are still in the world' (Heb. 13:3 NEB). In the churches I have served as pastor, it was a custom to sing after the baptism of a believer, 'Be thou faithful unto death, and I will give thee a crown of life' (Rev. 2:10 AV). In that setting, the congregation was saying to the young candidate, 'Be faithful to the Christ into whom you have been baptized, all the way through your life until you die.' Whether we interpret the words in that sense, or whether we interpret them in the original sense (for we may not assume that persecution will never be our lot) the demand and the promise of Jesus Christ 'the faithful and true witness' remains unchanged. 'Be faithful unto death, and I will give you the crown of life.'

Notes for chapter ten

1. T. H. Darlow, *The Upward Calling*, p.30.
2. Gerhard von Rad, *Genesis* (S.C.M., 1956), p.130.
3. H. E. Fosdick, *The Manhood of the Master* (S.C.M., 1918), p.47.
4. Order for Adult Baptism and Confirmation, *The Presbyterian Service Book* (The Publications Committee of the Presbyterian Church of England, 1968), p.57.

11 Gentleness

Gentleness and strength

The Greek word for the eighth of the nine fruits of the Spirit, *prautēs*, is variously translated into English as *meekness* (AV), *gentleness* (RSV, NEB, JB) and *humility* (GNB). No one of these words adequately translates *prautēs*, for today they all three carry a suggestion of weakness. Here is a pointer to the true meaning of the Greek word. John Charles, a former and famous soccer star of Leeds United and Wales, was often described by commentators and reporters as 'the gentle giant'. He was tall and massive, swift and powerful; but he didn't play a 'dirty' game. Out of consideration for his opponents, he kept his strength under control. This combination of strength and restraint, of power possessed but kept under control, and that out of regard for the welfare of others, is true gentleness.

Once we leave the strength out of gentleness, we get that unattractive caricature of it that the word *meekness* now suggests to us. Meekness is weakness. The meek man, so we imagine, is timid and feeble, spineless and incapable. He is lacking in energy and virility, in drive and aggression. He is the kind of person who wouldn't say boo to a goose – a doormat, exploited by all, who submits tamely to injury. No-one could possibly desire to be such a milk-and-watery person, such an ineffective creature.

The caricature versus the real thing can be illustrated from the character of Moses, the supreme example of meekness in the Old Testament. 'Now the man Moses was very meek, more than all men that were on the face of the earth'

(Nu. 12:3). It's this tribute which has given rise to the expression 'meek as Moses'. This popular phrase conveys the impression that Moses was soft and effeminate, flabby and weak, spineless and spiritless. What a travesty of the real Moses portrayed in the pages of the Pentateuch! There, as in Michelangelo's statue of Moses, he is a Titan, a person of superhuman size and strength. In his character we can see two characteristics of meekness as understood in the Bible.

Moses was meek towards God. It's in that context that he is said to be 'very meek, more than all men'. He wasn't concerned for himself or his own position, but only for God and the people's good. He depended on God; he had a trustful attitude to God; he was humbly obedient to God's will. Meekness is humility before God. Such are the characteristics of those who in the Old Testament are called the poor, the lowly, the meek. Oppressed by men, they look to God as their champion. The meek are the pious Israelites who, aware of their entire dependence on the Lord, submit to his will, and set their hope on him for salvation.

The meekness of Moses is also seen in his attitude *to the people*. His was the gentleness of strength controlled. By nature, Moses was hasty and impetuous, a man of hot temper and strong passions. He struck down the oppressor, and he struck the rock twice, with anger (Ex. 2:12; Nu. 20:11). Yet despite these occasional outbursts of passion, his powerful feelings were habitually controlled by his compassion and concern for the people. 'The nobler meekness is that which comes forth victorious from the struggle with strong emotion, and wins a glory from the passion it has subdued.'[1] True gentleness is strength brought under control. That is part of the meaning of *prautēs* in Greek usage. 'It is the regular word for an animal which has been domesticated, which has been trained to obey the word of command, which has learned to answer the reins.'[2] A cart-horse is just as strong after it has been 'broken-in' as it was before; but its great strength is now under control, and is put to good use. The gentle man is just as strong as the man of violence, but his strength is bridled. It is controlled by concern for others and directed to their welfare. It's this combination of strength and gentleness

174

which, according to the poet Tennyson, constitutes manliness,

> Gentleness, which, when it weds with manhood,
> Makes the man.

The Lion and the Lamb

Because the strength has been taken out of his gentleness, the character of Jesus Christ has often been grossly misrepresented. The image of Jesus in the minds of many is that of a person soft and sentimental. Several groups have contributed their quota to this distortion. Some parents have made a lasting impression on their children, by teaching them to pray to 'Gentle Jesus, meek and mild'. Artists have portrayed him as effeminate. In a typical picture he is clothed in white, sad-faced, hair perfectly groomed, his delicate hands cuddling a woolly lamb. Some of his biographers, such as Renan, have contributed to the caricature. 'Tenderness of heart was in him transfigured into infinite sweetness, vague poetry, universal charm.' This saccharine interpretation has been favoured by some teachers and preachers. They have upset the balance of his character by over-emphasizing his tenderness, gentleness and affection, while neglecting to speak of his courage, indignation and sternness. The gentleness of Christ ought not to be taken out of the context of the other counter-balancing virtues of his personality.

The apostle Paul writes about 'the meekness (*prautēs*) and gentleness (*epieikeia*) of Christ' (2 Cor. 10:1). The two words describe the attitude of Jesus, during his life on earth, to God and to people. They refer to the inner disposition of his mind, and to the outer quality of his relationships. Towards God, Jesus was meek. He was submissive before him, dependent on him, devoted to him. As a result, in his relationships with people, he was gentle and considerate. To those who were bearing the heavy burden of the law of Moses plus all the scribal elaborations and additions to it, he gave the gracious invitation; 'Take my yoke upon you, and learn from me; for I am gentle and lowly in heart, and you will find rest for your souls' (Mt. 11:29). To all those who come to him Jesus is a gentle teacher, patient with those slow to learn, kind to those

175

who stumble. He doesn't make hard and impossible demands of those who are loyal to him; for love makes hard tasks easy, heavy burdens light.

That Jesus was gentle and considerate, with children and women, with the sick and the outcasts, with friend and with foe, is apparent in many of the stories in the gospels. To characterize this aspect of his ministry as a whole, we may, like Matthew, apply to him the words of the first Song of the Servant (Is. 42:1-4; Mt. 12:18-21). There was nothing blatant and self-assertive about his methods. Quietly and unobtrusively he went about, exercising a ministry of sympathy and encouragement. His strength lay in his gentleness.

Strength and gentleness. In a remarkable vision given to John on Patmos, these two are combined and identified. The seer, looking into heaven, weeps when no creature in heaven is able to open the scroll on which the destiny of mankind is written. Then he is told to dry his tears, for there is One in heaven who can open the scroll, the Lion of the tribe of Judah, who has already conquered. But when John looks for the Lion, he sees the Lamb! The lion is the symbol of the sceptre, the ruler promised to Judah (Gn. 49:9-10). He stands for strength, majesty, regality. The lamb is the symbol of sacrifice. The Suffering Servant of the Lord, 'wounded for our transgressions, bruised for our iniquities' is likened to 'a lamb that is led to the slaughter' (Is. 53:5,7). The prophet Jeremiah also likens himself to 'a *gentle* lamb led to the slaughter' (Je. 11:19). He is a type of the Lamb of God, innocent, pure, meek; the sacrificial lamb who takes away the sin of the world. So John looks for the Lion, the king in his strength and majesty, and he sees 'a Lamb with the marks of slaughter upon him' (Rev. 5:6 NEB). He sees the Risen Christ who was crucified, the gentle and pure sacrificial Lamb, the Suffering Servant of God, who died and was raised to life for us. He reigns through his sacrifice. His regality is his gentleness. The Lion is the Lamb.

Considerateness .

Paul refers not only to the meekness, but also to the gentleness (*epieikeia*) of Christ (2 Cor. 10:1). There is no one English word that will give an adequate rendering of that Greek word. Here are some of the English words which have been used to translate it – moderation, forbearance, gentleness, courtesy, consideration, kindness. Perhaps Matthew Arnold's phrase *sweet-reasonableness* is as good as any. It has two characteristics. The man who has this quality of character is considerate towards others, and he does not necessarily insist on his own rights.

The gentle man is thoughtful and reasonable. When dealing with others he takes all the circumstances into consideration, and makes allowances for them. The considerate man may be contrasted with the man of strict justice who insists upon his legal rights. Aristotle (in the *Nicomachean Ethics*) speaks of *epieikeia* as better than justice; it interprets, applies and modifies the written law by looking to the spirit and not to the letter. For what is legally right can in some circumstances be morally wrong. Laws are necessarily general. That deficiency can be corrected when consideration is given to and allowance made for special circumstances.

A woman caught in the act of adultery was brought to Christ for judgment. The law of Moses laid it down that such a woman should be stoned to death. Jesus knew 'that in the course of justice none of us should see salvation'.[3] He went beyond legal justice, forgave her and sent her away with the command to sin no more (Jn. 8:1-11). With God 'mercy seasons justice'. The gentle man, himself a recipient of divine mercy, deals justly; but he often goes beyond justice out of consideration for the needs and circumstances of others.

Such a gentle man does not necessarily insist on his own rights. He is prepared to waive his undoubted rights if that appears to be the best thing to do in the situation. Jesus proved that he and his disciples were exempt from the temple poll tax; but to avoid giving needless offence, he then proceeded to pay it (Mt. 17:24-27). Would it not be preferable for you to be wronged, asks Paul, than to stand up for your rights, by taking your fellow-Christians to a court of law? (1 Cor. 6:1-8). When the pioneer missionary, Hudson Taylor, was working in China, one of his Chinese helpers made off with some of his books, money and furniture. He knew where the man and the goods were. He considered the matter carefully and decided not to take the man to court. Paul the missionary insisted on his rights on some occasions (*e.g.* Acts 16:36-37); but in most situations he was prepared to waive them. He proved from Scripture and everyday life that he had a right to be maintained by the churches he established and served. He waived this undoubted right so that he could preach the gospel free of charge (1 Cor. 9:1-18). He acted out of consideration for the welfare of others and the progress of the gospel. This attitude is worth bearing in mind, in an age when we are hypersensitive about our rights, with no corresponding emphasis on our responsibilities. In contemporary society we insist that each person has the right to his or her own opinion, and that all citizens have the right of free speech. The worker has a right to work, or, if unemployed, to be supported by the state. The student, it is believed, has a right to a grant, to be maintained while he studies at the taxpayers' expense. The sick have a right to medical treatment, and pensioners to various exemptions and privileges. A family with a low income has the right to 'supplementary benefits'. None of these rights should be taken for granted, and where possible, each one should be linked with the corresponding responsibility. There may be times when some of our rights should be modified or even surrendered, out of consideration for others. The gentle man, then, is a person who acts with due consideration for the feelings of others, tempers justice with mercy and does not always insist on his rights.

Tenderness

Being considerate and yielding to others does not mean that the gentle person is to be soft and spiritless. That would be to take the strength out of gentleness. According to Martin Luther King, Christians should be both tough-minded and tender-hearted. 'Jesus reminds us that the good life combines the toughness of the serpent and the tenderness of the dove. To have serpentine qualities devoid of dovelike qualities is to be passionless, mean and selfish. To have dovelike without serpentine qualities is to be sentimental, anaemic and aimless. We must combine strongly marked antitheses.'[4] Some teachers maintain that a man should be tough towards himself and tender towards others. That is not the right combination. Neurotic illness among Christians is sometimes due to the fact that they have been too gentle to others and too tough on themselves. I am required to be both gentle and stern towards myself, and other people, as the occasion demands. Without overlooking this need for both, we are concerned here with the *emotion* associated with gentleness, tender love towards others.

One of the most powerful drives in human nature is the parental or, as it is called in a mother, the maternal instinct. This impels a mother or a father to cherish and protect their offspring with tender love. It is in terms of this parental instinct, and the emotion of tenderness that goes with it, that Paul writes of his pastoral care for his converts at Thessalonica. 'We were gentle when we were with you, like a mother taking care of her children. Because of our love for you we were ready to share with you not only the Good News from God but even our own lives. You were so dear to us!' The same tenderness of heart is then described in terms of the other parent. 'You know that we treated each one of you just as a father treats his own children' (1 Thes. 2:7-8, 11 GNB).

The tender-heartedness of husbands and wives to their children should be the outcome and overflow of such a love for each other. Marriage is a spring; from it flows the love of parents to children, and of the whole family to the people beyond it. It isn't God's intention that the wife and mother should have a monopoly on this tender love. Mentally and spiritually there is no absolute difference between the sexes. The hundred per cent male or female are figments of the imagination: there are feminine characteristics in the man and masculine characteristics in the woman. Tender love in the husband and father is as necessary as it is in the wife and mother yet, in fact, it's often lacking in men. It is to husbands that Peter finds it necessary to write, 'live considerately with your wives'; and it is to fathers that Paul writes, 'do not provoke your children to anger' (1 Pet. 3:7; Eph. 6:4). In contemporary society, with the emphasis on toughness, there is plenty of evidence that not all men appreciate the importance of tenderness in marriage. Yet the sexual impulse can function properly, not in isolation, but only in an atmosphere and relationship of tenderness. This tender love should permeate the daily round of the couple and be diffused through the whole marital relationship. Gentleness is one colour in the rainbow of love, and, like charity, it should begin at home.

Gentle restoration

Gentleness should not be confined to relationships within the home. For those who live in accordance with the character and conduct of Christ will endeavour to seek the lost and restore the fallen, in a spirit of gentleness. Many stories in the gospels illustrate the love of Jesus for those who were outside the pale. The friend of tax-gatherers and sinners, he associated with dubious characters. He accepted as companions at table those who were ostracized by the religious. To those who needed him most and were conscious of their need he offered friendship, health and salvation.

This attitude of love towards the erring is underlined by the apostle Paul. 'Brethren, if a man is overtaken in any trespass, you who are spiritual should restore him in a spirit of gentleness' (Gal. 6:1). As the collect has it, 'by reason of the frailty of our nature we cannot always stand upright'. Any Christian can be caught off his guard, can slip up unintentionally, can be surprised and overcome by sin. When this happens, the mature members of the fellowship should endeavour to restore the offender. That word *restore* is used elsewhere of repairing a net or setting a bone. Correction should be positive and constructive. The aim is to put the dislocated member back into his rightful place. And this enterprise is to be undertaken 'in a spirit of gentleness'. The repair man is not to be harsh and censorious. On the contrary, he is to act in the spirit of 'there but for the grace of God go I'. Let him realize his own moral frailty and be on the alert against temptation. 'Look to yourself', repair man, 'lest you too be tempted' (Gal. 6:1).

It's significant that the apostle defined maturity, 'you who are spiritual', in terms of tenderness. Whether or not we are gentle is to be seen in our attitude to wrongdoers, whether within or outside the church. What is your attitude when, say, a member of your own family or of your church goes off the rails? The popular press provides abundant evidence of the salacious delight many people take in scandal. One of the most unattractive aspects of our human nature is the secret pleasure we may have in the downfall of another; perhaps because by comparison we are made to feel morally superior. But 'love is never glad when others go wrong' (1 Cor. 13:6 Moffatt). The mature Christian is saddened and grieved. If at all possible, he will seek out the one who has erred and endeavour to restore her or him in a spirit of gentleness. In this way, the restorer follows in the steps of him who came 'to seek and to save the lost' (Lk. 19:10).

Win others by gentleness

The virtue of gentleness is important, not only in the recovery of those who have lapsed from the fellowship, but also in winning to the fellowship those who are outside it. Those who are, and always have been, outside the Christian community can best be won for Christ and brought into the company of his disciples by those who speak and act in a spirit of gentleness. The apostles Peter and Paul, as is clear from their letters, were concerned with the attitude of Christians to those outside their number. Unfortunately, a Christian can make a bad impression on a non-Christian. He can live and speak in such a way that the unbeliever is not attracted but repelled. Such a Christian, conscious of possessing the truth, may become over-confident and overbearing. Dogmatic and aggressive in stating his convictions, he may refuse to listen with interest and respect to what the other person has to say. He can be, at best, superior and patronizing, and at worst, self-righteous and censorious in his attitude to those who are outside the church. Aggressive and belligerent, he acts like a soldier in battle rather than like a lover wooing and winning the beloved. The unbeliever, to him, is an enemy to be conquered, and evangelism is a military campaign.

As over against this negative, the two great apostles inculcate a positive attitude to those who are not Christians. The sincere convictions and moral standards of unbelievers are to be respected and, as far as possible, believers are to live peaceably with them (Rom. 12:17-18). Christians should avoid conduct which inclines unbelievers to question their sanity! They should combine the characteristics of the serpent and the dove, be both wary and sincere, prudent and pure in motive – 'wise as to what is good and guileless as to what is evil' (Rom. 16:19). If disputes with unbelievers arise Christians should not always insist on their rights. Thus, they will avoid the quarrelling which more than anything else repels the potential convert. Far better 'to be gentle, and to show perfect courtesy toward all men' (Tit. 3:2). This conciliatory attitude is especially important in the Christian pastor. He 'must not be quarrelsome but kindly to every one, an apt teacher, forbearing, correcting his opponents with gentleness. God may perhaps grant that they will repent and come to know the truth' (2 Tim. 2:24-25). 'Perhaps' – it's not certain; but it's likely that gentleness will succeed.

Shortly before the outbreak of the persecution instigated by Nero, the relationship of Christians to pagans was exceptionally delicate and important. Such was the situation in which the apostle Peter appealed to believers to witness with gentleness. If you should be called upon to suffer for Christ's sake, he writes, consider yourselves happy. Instead of fearing those who trouble you, enthrone Christ as Lord in the sanctuary of your hearts. Always be ready to give an intelligent account (*apologia*) to anyone who asks you why you are a Christian, 'yet do it with gentleness and reverence' (1 Pet. 3:14-15). The apostle is concerned both with what the Christian says and with the way he says it. The *apologia* should be a reasonable and meaningful account of the Christian faith and hope. It should be given with courtesy to the enquirer who asks for it, and with all due reverence for the mystery of the gospel from the witness who makes the explanation. Like Jesus, the gentle Christian will have an intense interest in and concern for each individual, and will deal with each one appropriately.

Gentleness triumphant

We have just seen that the restoration of the lapsed and erring, and the winning of unbelievers, are best done by those of a gentle spirit. It's possible to extend the application of this truth to other activities. There are many things which can be done by gentleness, which cannot be done well, or even done at all, by force. That's the moral in the fable of the quarrel between the wind and the sun. Said the wind to the sun, 'I'm stronger than you. I'll prove it. Let's see which of us can make that ploughman take off his coat.' So the wind blew hard, but all his blowing could not drag the coat away. 'Now', said the sun gently, 'let me try.' He beamed, and soon the man exclaimed, 'How hot it is!' Then he unbuttoned his coat. Presently he threw it open; and at last, off came the coat.[5] Force incites resistance. It may be possible to achieve by warmth and gentleness that which cannot be done by aggression and violence. We have emphasized the truth that gentleness and strength belong together. We must now go further and identify them. In many situations gentleness *is* strength.

The Bible links gentleness and dominion; by the action of God the one leads to the other. Men of pride and power will soon disappear; the future belongs to the humble and poor. 'A little while, and the wicked will be no more...but the humble shall possess the land' (Ps. 37:10-11 NEB). God himself removes the arrogant and establishes the lowly. 'I will remove everyone who is proud and arrogant, and you will never again rebel against me on my sacred hill. I will leave there a humble and lowly people, who will come to me for help' (Zp. 3:11-12 GNB). As the representative of that humble and oppressed remnant, Mary, in the *Magnificat*, celebrates the great reversal which the birth of Jesus will bring about. 'He has brought down mighty kings from their thrones, and lifted up the lowly' (Lk. 1:52 GNB). In the third beatitude,

Jesus underlines this Old Testament hope and promise. 'How blest are those of a gentle spirit; they shall have the earth for their possession' (Mt. 5:5 NEB). The gentle don't conquer the earth: they inherit it. Sons of God, they receive the earth from their Father, as gift and legacy.

This hope of inheriting the earth is partly realized and partly deferred. Already, in this life, the gentle possess the earth. They may own very little of it, but they do possess it. For we possess that which we appreciate and love. Paul, for example, refers to himself 'as having nothing, and yet possessing everything' (2 Cor. 6:10). The apostle had no material possessions, yet he possessed the treasures of wisdom and knowledge, and the riches of friendship and fellowship. The gentle Francis of Assisi owned nothing; yet he possessed brother sun and sister water, creation and all its creatures, inanimate, animate and human – by loving them. To a land-owner a humble peasant said, 'You own the land, but I possess the landscape.' Of course, we can also possess what we own, but happy are they who possess what they don't own. 'All things are yours' (1 Cor. 3:21). Because the humble appreciate the earth and love the people on it, they inherit it, in part, already.

But only in part – for the realized hope is deferred until the kingdom of Christ is established and fulfilled on the earth. In his portrait of the messianic kingdom, the prophet links humility with victory, gentleness with dominion. 'Lo, your king comes to you; triumphant and victorious is he, humble and riding on an ass.' Then the instruments of violence are destroyed, and peace is enthroned in a universal kingdom (Zc. 9:9-10). Christ entered Jerusalem, not like Judas Maccabaeus, on a war horse, but on an ass, symbol of royalty and peace. The Redeemer came not to coerce but to persuade. He is the king who rules in the strength of gentleness, in the power of sacrificial love. When and where this gentle reign of Christ is accepted, by individuals and by communities, there and then the meek are inheriting the earth. When he comes in glory it is not to change the character of his reign. He will be the same tomorrow as he was yesterday. He will not exchange gentleness for force, persuasion for coercion.

'Omnipotence is not to be understood as the power of un-limited coercion, but as the power of infinite persuasion, the invincible power of self-negating, self-sacrificing love.'[6] The Messiah overcomes his enemies by the way of the cross. The Lion *is* the Lamb; and with him the gentle strong will inherit the earth.

Notes for chapter eleven

1. J. Hastings, *The Greater Men and Women of the Bible* (T. and T. Clark, 1914), vol. 2, p.299.
2. W. Barclay, *Daily Bible Readings: Matthew* (Committee on Publications, Church of Scotland, 1956), p.91.
3. William Shakespeare, *Merchant of Venice*.
4. Matthew 10:16; Martin Luther King, *Strength to Love* (Hodder and Stoughton, 1964), p.5.
5. H. L. Gee, *Tales to Tell Again* (Epworth, 1955), p.144.
6. G. B. Caird, *Revelation* (A. and C. Black, 1965), p.75.

12 Self-control

Athletes in training

'The fruit of the Spirit is...self-control.' Paul himself illustrates this ninth virtue. Writing to the Christians at Corinth, where the Isthmian Games were held every three years, he likens himself to a runner and a boxer. Before the contests, every athlete had to submit to a rigorous discipline. For ten months he was under oath to keep to a prescribed diet and a strenuous course of training. When the time came to compete, the athlete was completely fit. In the foot race, where there could be only one winner, the utmost effort was necessary. In the boxing bouts the pugilist couldn't win by wasting his punches on the air! His opponent could be knocked out only by forceful and well-placed blows. The Greek athlete accepted this discipline and made this all-out effort in order to win a crown of laurel leaves that withered within a few days. Paul applies the illustration to himself. Like the runner, he is stretching every nerve in the race of life and pressing onwards to the finishing line. Like the boxer, he pommels and hardens his opponent, his body, and brings it under his control, lest in the contest of life he should be disqualified (1 Cor. 9:24-27).

In this picture of the two athletes there are five insights into the nature of self-control. The athlete has a positive purpose – to win fame. Christian discipline isn't negative. Its aim is fitness for the service of God. To achieve that purpose the Christian, like the athlete, must go into training and submit to a strict discipline. 'Keep yourself in training for a godly life. Physical exercise has some value, but spiritual exercise is valuable in every way, because it promises life both for the present and for the future' (1 Tim. 4:7-8 GNB). If that discipline is to be effective, it must include every aspect of life. 'Every athlete practises self-restraint *all round*' (1 Cor. 9:25 Moffatt). That which has to be controlled and mastered is named. 'I pommel *my body* and subdue it.' Finally, both in the training and in the actual contest, the Christian, like the athlete, must put all he's got into it. Then, having 'finished the race', and having 'fought the good fight', he will receive the unfading crown of life eternal (2 Tim. 4:7-8). We shall take up these five aspects, beginning with the fourth.

The body: temple not tomb

The body to be controlled is not a tomb; it is a temple of the Holy Spirit. To Plato and the Greeks the body was regarded as the tomb in which the soul was imprisoned. The task of philosophy, or of asceticism, was to free the soul from the body to which it was shackled, and by which it was contaminated. As aspects of man's bodily life, the senses, the appetites and the passions were deprecated and regarded with loathing and hostility. Where this attitude to the body is adopted, the task of discipline will be misunderstood and misdirected.

'Gin a body meet a body, Coming through the rye; Gin a body kiss a body, Need a body cry?' Robert Burns uses the word *body* as it is used in the Bible; a body is a person. Self-control is the control of the self, the whole person. It isn't only or mainly the physical aspect of our human nature that has to be controlled. Five only, out of the fifteen 'works of the flesh' refer to the physical appetites (Gal. 5:19-21). *The flesh*, as used by Paul in this context, is our total human nature as weakened and corrupted by sin. The phrase applies to the whole personality and not just to its physical aspects. Elsewhere Paul refers to the 'sensuous *mind*' (Col. 2:18). The mind of a person has to be disciplined as well as his appetites. Indeed, the discipline of the outer life depends on the prior discipline of the inner life. 'For from within, out of the heart of man, come evil thoughts' (Mk. 7:21). The 'works of the flesh' spring from the heart. Take for example the conscience which, according to Thomas Aquinas, is 'the mind making moral judgments'. The unenlightened and undisciplined conscience of man has been responsible for some of the most appalling atrocities and crimes in history. We need to control the censorious Pharisee in us as well as the licentious publican. In short, there is no part of the body, *i.e.* the whole person, which is exempt from the need for control.

That's not to deny that the physical aspect of our human nature also needs to be 'pommelled and subdued', not because our physical make-up is evil in itself, but because it has become enemy-occupied territory. Sin has invaded and occupied the frail body of flesh and blood, and from that base wages war against the soul (1 Pet. 2:11). Our instincts and appetites make demands on us for immediate satisfaction. Those demands are often strong and urgent, hot and imperious. Uncontrolled, they are dangerous and destructive. With some of these drives, *e.g.* for food, for drink, for sex, we shall be concerned in more detail. None of these drives, however, is evil in itself. Some Christians suffer needless conflict, tension and inner distress because they insist upon regarding as 'common and unclean' that which God has created and will cleanse. A sane and healthy attitude to the instincts and appetites of the body is essential to self-control: for we can control only that which we accept. A Christian is called to be Christ's athlete, accepting, controlling and consecrating all the powers of his human nature; not a morbid ascetic trying to root out or disown the natural impulses. 'Do not yield your members to sin as instruments of wickedness, but yield yourselves to God as men who have been brought from death to life, and your members to God as instruments of righteousness' (Rom. 6:13). The body can be kept as the Lord has already made it – a temple of the Holy Spirit (1 Cor. 6:19).

Self-restraint all round

Once we have accepted the truth that the body to be controlled is the whole person, we are in a better position to appreciate a second point in Paul's description of the athlete. 'Every athlete exercises self-control *in all things*'...'he practises self-restraint *all round*'. We can fail to achieve self-control just because we don't attempt all-round discipline. We may, misguided, concentrate on one narrow aspect of life and ignore others of equal or greater importance. Perhaps, for example, a woman has a long struggle with her temper, which she vainly tries to control. Although she makes heroic efforts to restrain it, she fails again and again. One reason may be that she is trying too hard to gain mastery in too narrow a sphere, and thus concentrating her attention upon the very thing she wishes to avoid. She would be well advised to practise 'self-restraint all round'. Does she, for example, get up in the morning at the right time, or eat temperately at table, or restrain her sexual desires, or discipline her tongue? Self-control practised in any part of life helps one to achieve self-control in every other part. A fortified position in the enemy line may be out-flanked where direct attack would fail. A particular weakness is best overcome, not by direct assault, but by the practice of an all-round discipline.

There's another unfortunate consequence of concentrating discipline on one or two specific issues. In that very concentration we may be ignoring other aspects of life where self-control may be no less, and perhaps even more necessary. Take, for example, the unfortunate modern tendency to restrict temperance to the question of drink. 'It helps people to forget that you can be just as intemperate about lots of other things. A man who makes his golf or his motor-bicycle the centre of his life, or a woman who devotes all her thoughts to clothes or bridge or her dog, is being just as "intemperate" as someone who gets drunk every evening.'[1] Mrs Grundy may be strict on matters of sexual morality, and yet make no attempt at all to control her own tongue. Discipline is distorted if we become over-strict about some things and over-indulgent about others. This distortion can be corrected by recognition of the need for all-round discipline.

Folk-lore and history underline this truth. Thetis, mother of Achilles, dipped her child in the waters of the river Styx, by which he became invulnerable, except for that part of the heel by which she held him. The bravest of the Greeks, he overcame every foe; until eventually he was slain by the arrow of Paris, which pierced his heel. He was overcome at his weak point, his only vulnerable spot. The Jebusites, confident of the impregnability of Jerusalem, jeered at David and his army. 'You will never get in here; even the blind and the crippled could keep you out.' But David, who had discovered the Achilles' heel of Jerusalem, said to his soldiers, 'Go up through the water tunnel' (2 Sa. 5:6-8 GNB). With a like strategy Cyrus of Persia captured the city of Sardis. The battlements of the citadel overlooking an unscalable cliff were left unguarded. A Persian captain, Hyeroeades, and his commandos, scaled the cliff and captured the city. We need to garrison the walls of our citadel all the way round. The moral of these stories is, in the words of Charles Wesley's hymn, 'leave no unguarded place'.

Nothing to excess

We pass on now from self-control (*egkrateia*) to temperance. There is a difference. We recall that in the teaching of Plato and in subsequent Greek ethical thought, there are four cardinal virtues: wisdom, courage, justice and temperance. Here, the fourth virtue, temperance (*sōphrosynē*) means moderation. It has reference to pleasures, appetites, desires. The man of sound sense doesn't go to excess in his enjoyment of the pleasures and satisfactions of life. He goes to the right length and no further. His guideline for conduct is 'nothing too much'. There are a few traces of this idea in the Wisdom Books of the Bible and the Apocrypha, which may have been influenced by Greek thought. For example: 'So don't be too good or too wise – why kill yourself?' (Ec. 7:16 GNB). This principle from pagan ethics should be accepted with caution and criticism. The author of Ecclesiastes seems to quote it as something to be deplored rather than imitated. As we have already seen in chapter two, in some respects it is contrary to the teaching and example of Christ. On the one hand, if a thing is inherently wrong, it cannot be right to do it at all, even in strict moderation. On the other hand, there are some virtues (*e.g.* caring, giving) which *should* be carried to excess. With this warning and these qualifications, however, moderation can be a useful guideline, especially for the control of the appetites. Indeed, even emotions and affections, good in themselves, can be embarrassing and unhelpful if expressed without restraint. Overwhelmed with tender feelings for his newly-found brother Benjamin, Joseph was about to break down in public. He withdrew into the privacy of his room and wept there. He returned to the company when he was in control of himself (Gn. 43:31). The gushing and sentimental person tends to overdo the expression of sympathy, affection and appreciation. There are virtues which can be carried to excess, unless they are checked and counter-balanced by their complementaries. As we have seen in the character of Christ, one virtue can be complemented and therefore moderated by another. Excess of zeal, for example, could become fanaticism, unless moderated by wisdom, serenity and compassion. This is the moderation, not of the mediocre, but of the balanced character.

There is one particular aspect of contemporary life in which the avoidance of extremes is of great importance. For a healthy and satisfying life, both rest and work are necessary. Either can be carried to excess. Sloth, one of the Seven Deadly Sins, is an inordinate and constant desire for bodily rest and sleep. It's an ancient vice. 'How long will you lie there, O sluggard? When will you arise from your sleep?' Indolence leads to poverty, yet it is difficult to rouse the lazy man, for he can always find a ready excuse for his idleness. He should go to the anthill and watch the little creatures busily at work, preparing for the coming winter (Pr. 6:6-11). Nowadays, in the Welfare State, where the incentive of fear has been weakened and indolence doesn't necessarily lead to poverty, the temptation to idleness has been strengthened. Some succumb to it. At the other extreme are those who work to excess. There are workaholics as well as alcoholics. For a worker can become emotionally dependent on his work, seeking from it not only a livelihood and prosperity, but also security, self-esteem and status. The work becomes a drug on which the worker is hooked, a compulsion beyond his control. He finds it difficult to stop, and if he stops, is restless and dissatisfied. In the ministry of Christ we see the principle of alternation. He withdrew from activity to rest; he went forth from rest to work (Mk. 6:31). As regards both work and rest, the Spirit enables us to be temperate, to go to the right length and no further.

Food and drink

It's when we turn to eating and drinking that the principle of moderation, of nothing to excess, is most useful as a guide. God created the exquisite pleasure of eating, and those who follow the example of 'the Son of man' who 'came eating and drinking' will accept this pleasure with gratitude. The glutton perverts this natural function by making the pleasurable sensations which normally accompany eating an end in themselves. Although written over three centuries ago, it would be difficult to improve on Jeremy Taylor's four guidelines for temperance in eating.[2] *'Eat not before the time.'* Wait for your regular meals. *'Eat not hastily and impatiently.'* Civilized men should not gobble food voraciously, like vultures or wolves. Eating should be a human, not an animal act. Appetite should be joined to the mental powers of discernment and choice. Taste can transform eating into an experience, a personal act. *'Eat not delicately or nicely.'* He is referring to the gluttony of *quality* not quantity: that of the gourmet who has an inordinate love for delicate fare, a finicky obsession with food of the highest quality. *'Eat not too much.'* This is the gluttony of *quantity*: that of the greedy man who habitually eats more food than he needs. Over-eating has not only physical, but also mental and spiritual repercussions. It induces a dull and heavy state of mind, a lack of awareness and sensitivity in personal relationships, a state of torpor in which worship is virtually impossible. As with the workaholic, the glutton may be using food as a drug, as a means of escape from the tensions and demands of life. A useful guideline is, 'always rise from the table feeling that you would like a little more.' Or as Ben-Sira puts it in the Apocrypha, 'A little is quite enough for a well-bred person…a moderate diet ensures sound sleep…be moderate in all your activities' (Ecclus. 31:19-20, 27 JB).

The same advice is given for drinking. 'Wine is life for man if drunk in moderation. What is life worth without wine? It was created to make men happy. Drunk at the right time and in the right amount, wine makes for a glad heart and a cheerful mind. Bitterness of soul comes of wine drunk to excess out of temper or bravado' (Ecclus. 31:27-29 JB). For the Psalmist, to whom Ben-Sira here refers, 'wine to gladden the heart of man' is the gift of God, and the acceptance and enjoyment of this gift was a normal part of life in Israel of old (Ps. 104:15). Jesus continued in this tradition. He could not have been misrepresented and slandered as 'a drunkard' unless he had been in the habit of drinking wine (Mt. 11:19). And fermented wine at that, capable of bursting old wine-skins! His first miracle was the transformation of water into wine at a wedding, and he blessed and shared a cup of wine with his disciples at the Last Supper.

Alongside this grateful acceptance of God's gift, there is another attitude to wine in the Scriptures. Drunkenness is widely condemned, and the dangers of over-indulgence in drink are emphasized. 'Show me someone who drinks too much...and I will show you someone miserable and sorry for himself....Don't let wine tempt you, even though it is rich red, though it sparkles in the cup, and it goes down smoothly. The next morning you will feel as if you had been bitten by a poisonous snake' (Pr. 23:29, 31-32 GNB). These warnings are continued in the New Testament (Gal. 5:21; Eph. 5:18). Some Christians, having these and other Scriptures in mind, take the view that all drinking of intoxicating liquors is evil. For them, temperance is total abstinence. This conviction is strengthened by their observation of the consequences of drinking in contemporary society. For one thing, drinking in moderation is not possible for some people: they slide easily and almost inevitably into excess. There are the alcoholics, tens of thousands of them. The number is on the increase. They are sick, hooked, enslaved. There are the drunken drivers, and all the lives maimed or lost on the roads. Drink lowers resistance to temptation, and is responsible for much sexual immorality and violence, *e.g.* the hooliganism of some football supporters. It's a colossal waste of money, and of foodstuffs in a hungry world. These facts should be taken into serious consideration by any Christian seeking to make up his or her mind about whether to drink in moderation or to be a total abstainer.

In addition to these grim facts, consideration should be given to the the principle enunciated by Paul. 'You should decide never to do anything that would make your brother stumble or fall into sin' (Rom. 14:13 GNB). It may be possible for me to drink in moderation, but would my influence and example be a stumbling-block to some *other* person, who in this matter of drink may lack the gift of self-control? In some circumstances it may be the loving thing to give up one's Christian freedom out of consideration for the welfare of others. '"We are allowed to do anything" – but not everything is helpful. No one should be looking to his own interests, but to the interests of others' (1 Cor. 10:23-24 GNB). This principle itself should be set alongside the equally important principle of Christian liberty. For what things, innocent in themselves, don't prove harmful to some people? If the strong always give way to the scruples of the weak, they will have little Christian liberty left to enjoy. We are left with four guidelines. 1. In view of the teaching of Scripture and the example of Christ, we may enjoy God's good gifts in moderation. 2. We must always take into account the welfare of others, especially of the weaker brethren immediately around us. 3. In the light of these two principles, 'each one should firmly make up his own mind' (Rom. 14:5 GNB). 4. We should respect the convictions of those who may differ from us on this matter of moderation versus abstinence. 'So then, let us stop judging one another' (Rom. 14:13 GNB).

Controlling the tongue

The faculty of speech, which distinguishes man from the animal creation, is extremely difficult to control. 'Man is able to tame and has tamed all other creatures – wild animals and birds, reptiles and fish. But no one has ever been able to tame the tongue. It is evil and uncontrollable, full of deadly poison' (Jas. 3:7-8 GNB). Words are powerful. As the small bit controls the horse, and the little rudder the big ship, so the little tongue can do great things. Yet, with an inconsistency contrary to nature, those great achievements are sometimes good and sometimes evil. For with the same tongue we worship and give thanks to God, and cause havoc and destruction in our personal relationships (see Jas 3:1-12).

The sins of speech condemned in the New Testament are of four main kinds.

1. *Lying*   Falsehood must be put away. For deception breeds distrust and destroys the fellowship (Eph. 4:25).

2. *Dirty talk*   Foul language pollutes the speaker and the hearer. To some people it makes the grossest sin attractive and amusing. It should be replaced by words that build up the morals and character of those to whom they are addressed (Eph. 4:29).

3. *Insulting and abusive language*   This springs from anger and contempt for others (Mt. 5:21-22). A man who, in outbursts of temper, speaks abusive and insulting words is 'like a city broken into and left without walls' (Pr. 25:28). He is vulnerable, defenceless. But 'he who is slow to anger is better than the mighty, and he who rules his spirit than he who takes a city' (Pr. 16:32).

4. *Slander*   is character-assassination. Gossips, whisperers, scandalmongers, defamers, run down people in their absence. They do harm to the reputation of others behind their backs. 'A curse on the scandal-monger and the deceitful, he has ruined many who lived in concord. That third tongue has shaken many' (Ecclus. 28:13-14 JB). That third tongue – for according to the Talmud, slander makes three victims: the slanderer himself, the listener and the person slandered.

How does the Holy Spirit tame the tongue, which, according to James, no *man* can tame? Basically, by transforming our nature. To evil men Jesus said, 'How can you *say* good things when you *are* evil? For the mouth speaks what the heart is full of.' Good words come spontaneously from a heart made new. 'A good person brings good things out of his treasure of good things' (Mt. 12:34-35 GNB). While this transformation is taking place, the Christian has to exercise discipline, to practise controlling the tongue. This discipline is three-fold.

1. *Think*. Realizing the tremendous potential of words, for good or for evil, make a habit of thinking before speaking. How often we 'let slip' words we would do anything to recall. So exercise the negative discipline of restraint. We are warned in Scripture about the dangers of too much speech. Mr Talkative is not among the King's pilgrims. Don't talk too much. 'Lord, place a guard at my mouth, a sentry at the door of my lips' (Ps. 141:3 GNB).

2. *Speak the truth*. The apostle Paul says that it is by 'speaking the truth in love' that we grow up in every way into Christ (Eph. 4:15). Is it true? With that question we can test every utterance. It is not sufficient to avoid the deliberate lie; false impressions can be given by exaggeration, by distortion, by withholding all the facts, by quoting out of context. Accuracy in speech is more difficult than is commonly supposed, but it can be attained with practice. The Spirit of truth will enable the Christian to be the man who 'speaks truth from his heart' (Ps. 15:2).

3. *Speak the truth in love*. Is it kind? That can be the second positive test of every utterance. It's possible to speak the truth in an unkind way, to be brutally frank. The importance of kind words has been emphasized in the chapter on kindness. Reference has already been made to the evil of slander. Great harm can be done by the negative and destructive criticism of others in their absence. This sin of the tongue can be eliminated by observing a simple rule, 'I will not say in anyone's absence that which I would be unwilling to say in his presence.' There is a place for constructive criticism, but that should be made in private to the person concerned and

not to others in public. So here are the three guidelines: think before you speak, speak the truth and speak the truth in love.

Controlling sex

No less difficult than the control of the tongue, perhaps more so for most people, is the control of the sexual impulse. The strength and insistency of the appetite itself, the delay of marriage for economic or professional reasons, the stimulation of sex on the television, in the popular press, in advertisements, *etc.*, all contribute to make self-control in this sphere more difficult. There is no one simple answer to this problem. What has been said already about the other virtues, especially about love, patience, goodness, faithfulness, and what follows in the last two sections of this chapter, all bears indirectly on it. We shall be concerned directly with four things: with standards, with acceptance, with restraint and with love.

1. We should accept *the standards* and demands of sexual morality which we find in the teaching of Jesus and of the apostles. Chastity is the preservation of sexual integrity and purity, and this involves continence before marriage and fidelity in marriage. Like the invisible steel girders which support a lofty building, the virtue of self-control is supported and strengthened by firm convictions. Allow your moral standards to be eroded, and the incentive to control yourself is weakened. In this connection we need to be on our guard against those who change the labels. Pre-marital sex is fornication, and extra-marital sex is adultery, the former is condemned at least eighteen and the latter some fifteen times in the New Testament. The Spirit will supply the wisdom and strength to live according to these given and revealed guidelines.

2. Sex is the creation and gift of God, and should be *accepted* without shame and with gratitude (Gn. 1:27-28). It is easier to control that which we accept. The sexual impulse should not be regarded as a disreputable relative to be disowned,

still less as an enemy to be slain. It should be accepted as a friend and ally, which, rightly directed, enriches life and helps us to achieve the divine purpose. For it was God the Creator who set within us this basic instinct and its associated affections, which drives and draws most people into courtship, love and marriage. Outside of marriage, sexual emotion and desire can be expressed and sublimated in many of our activities, and as one ingredient within the sentiment of love, it may enter into and enrich many of our deep personal relationships. Within the commitment of marriage it is both for the procreation and continuance of the human race, and for the expression, enjoyment and fulfilment of personal love. Sharing themselves, husband and wife can grow steadily towards that wholeness, two becoming one, which is the primary purpose of marriage.

3. In most people, the sexual urge is strong and, when roused, is urgent, persistent and imperious. That's why discipline, strong and stringent, is essential. *Self-restraint* is as necessary as self-expression. We have to say *no* as well as *yes*. According to the teaching of Christ, this discipline must be inward as well as outward: it must include thought, imagination and desire, as well as word, deed and relationship. He carries the discipline of sex to the heart of man, beyond the outward act, to the first touch of the hand and the first glance of the eye. And beyond these to the first kindling of desire in the heart (Mt. 5:27-30). Plucking out the offending eye, cutting off the offending hand, is of course picture language. The Christian must be his own surgeon. He must cut out of his life all the occasions of evil, for instance in terms of eye and hand, pornographic pictures and literature, and excessive 'necking and petting'. He must incise any pleasure, recreation, habit, association, personal relationship, that leads to sin. To cut out, to deny, is sometimes necessary; but the purpose is always positive, to enter into fulness of life. For, of course, the heart cannot be kept pure just by cutting things out. The positive side of this discipline, filling the heart with that which is good, is touched upon in the last two sections of this chapter.

4. Self-control is the last in a list of virtues of which the first and inclusive virtue is *love*. Sex can best be controlled by love. Sexual desire and love are not identical, but the sexual impulse need not and should not be isolated from love. Sexual desire should be one ingredient in a larger whole, one colour in a many-coloured rainbow. The other ingredients are tenderness and affection, respect and submission, courtesy and consideration, the desire to protect and to cherish, the impulse to give and to care. This complex of emotions is, in the language of psychology, a sentiment, a learned attitude and *complex* emotional response towards some person. 'In the absence of sentiments our emotional life would be a mere chaos, without order, consistency or continuity of any kind; and all our social relations and conduct, being based on the emotions and their impulses, would be correspondingly chaotic, unpredictable and unstable. It is only through the systematic organization of the emotional dispositions in sentiments that the volitional control of the immediate prompting of the emotions is rendered possible.'[3] Within the sentiment of love, caring, the instincts and their associated emotions are controlled. When you really love a person who is sexually attractive to you, your relationship with that person, including the sexual ingredient in that relationship, is controlled by love. By kindling within us true love for people, the self-giving love which seeks the good of the other person, the Spirit imparts to us the gift of self-control. In the sphere of sex, the first fruit of the Spirit, love, includes the ninth, self-control.

Exercising self-control

In his description of the athlete, Paul emphasizes the necessity for both exercise and effort. 'Every athlete *exercises* self-control...every athlete practises self-restraint.' In the foot race 'only one receives the prize'. Therefore the utmost *effort* is necessary. There is no quick and easy way to the achievement of self-control. The athlete of Christ must go into training: the price of self-control is strenuous effort. 'Practice makes perfect.' That's a true saying, provided (as emphasized below) that the one who practises has already received the 'gift' to be improved and appropriated by practice. In the case of the athlete, in the period before the games, exercise and effort go together. In the spiritual contest it is daily exercise and effort that prepares the Christian for the big test. 'Keep the faculty of effort alive in you by a little gratuitous exercise every day. That is, be systematically ascetic or heroic in little unnecessary points, do every day or two something for no other reason than that you would rather not do it, so that when the hour of dire need draws nigh, it may find you not unnerved and untrained to stand the test.'[4] It's beyond doubt that the best preparation for the severe moral test is habitual obedience in lesser decisions. It was by all that went before the dread contest that Christ was finally victorious in dark Gethsemane.

Immediately after writing about the fruits of the Spirit, Paul appeals to the believers to 'walk by the Spirit' (Gal. 5:25). To walk is to put one foot in front of another. Progress is slow but sure. We best advance in self-control, not by attempting a great leap forward, but by taking one step at a time. Some people try to leap forward by making magnificent resolutions. The resolutions are soon broken and the outcome is discouragement. If those resolutions are idealistic, general and futuristic, they become a substitute for day-to-day obedience. The road to hell is paved with good resolutions. The steady practice of self-control is the better way. As muscles and limbs are strengthened by exercise, so passions are gradually mastered and virtues steadily appropriated by the practice of obedience. 'Both the spiritual and the bodily powers of a man increase and become perfected and strengthened by their exercise. By exercising your hand in writing, sewing, or knitting you will accustom it to such work; by frequently exercising yourself in composition you will learn to write easily and well; by exercising yourself in doing good works or in conquering your passions and temptations, you will in time learn to do good works easily and with delight: and with the help of God's all-active grace you will easily learn to conquer your passions.'[5] The Spirit works with us, and he creates and strengthens the virtue of self-control, as we make the effort. Practise self-control, not deterred by failures, getting up again at once after a fall, and pressing on with cheerful courage.

Controlled by Christ

The discipline of the athlete has a positive purpose. 'They do it to receive a perishable wreath', or rather, they do it for that of which the wreath is a symbol. They train for achievement, victory, fame. For the Christian, self-control and positive purpose are inseparable. We need to make right and active use of the strong drives within us. To do nothing is to ask for trouble. Plato likened the passions within us to lively horses drawing a chariot. A good driver will control, guide and use them, but he is not likely to succeed in keeping them inactive. Jesus warned his contemporaries of the perils of the empty, inactive, neutral life (Lk. 11:24-26). We are called to serve, to live *for* something, and to live for it strongly. We don't get the impression that the great characters of Scripture achieved self-control by 'sitting on the kettle-lid'. The heroes of faith were men of action. So while the immediate answer to an impulse must often be *no*, the long-term answer is to use in a right and positive way that same particular impulse and power.

It has been truly said that 'only a passion can master a passion'. The dynamic impulses of human nature can be controlled only by something stronger than themselves. In all ages some people have attempted to live the good life by obedience to ethical principles, or to a code of laws. But a code, as Paul knew from experience, was impotent against the hot, surging impulses of sin. Abstract ideals are notoriously powerless. The influence of a person, on the other hand, is by no means powerless. We see this in the hero-worship of the adolescent. Then the ideal is no longer inert, remote and abstract; rather, it evokes and engages the emotions as well as the assent of the mind. In this phenomenon we have some indication of what happens when Jesus Christ is enthroned in the heart and is admired, loved and worshipped. The whole personality, the body, passes under the control of a powerful ideal, powerful because personal.

Powerful, because engaging the emotions and affections as well as the mind and will. Powerful, because not remote but near. But we cannot leave it there. Jesus is not merely a hero who engages our passions like a pop star. When Jesus is enthroned, the strong is mastered by the stronger; the passions by a dominant passion (Lk. 11:24-26).

For the Christian, then, self-control is really Christ-control. When Christ rules over us, we experience what a former professor of moral philosophy, Thomas Chalmers, called 'the expulsive power of a new affection'. Paul says, 'I am *controlled* by the love of Christ' (2 Cor. 5:14 Moffatt). Self-control is the fruit of the Holy Spirit. It is received from Christ as we surrender our lives to him. And as he lives in us and rules over us, he produces in us this good quality, and all the other fruits of the Spirit. To be the master of myself I must be the servant of Christ. In his service I may find the freedom which is the ultimate reward of discipline. 'Make me a captive, Lord, and then I shall be free.'[6] With great simplicity, Jeremy Taylor expresses the positive purpose of all Christian self-control: 'Let my body be a servant of my spirit, and both body and spirit be servants of Jesus.'

Notes for chapter twelve

1. C. S. Lewis, *Mere Christianity* (Collins, 1952), p.72.
2. Jeremy Taylor, *Holy Living* (Griffin, Farran and Co.), chap. 2, section 2.
3. W. McDougall, *Social Psychology* (Methuen, 1919), pp. 159-160.
4. W. James, *The Principles of Psychology* (1890), vol. 1, chap. 4.
5. J. I. Sergieff, *Thoughts and Counsels* (1899), p.305.
6. George Matheson.

Postscript

The end of this book can be the beginning of an adventure. I take up again into this postscript the little word *how* used in the preface. *How* has to do with ways and means, not with aims and goals. The end of the Christian life has been painted for us in glowing colours in the gospels, the portraits of our Lord Jesus Christ. We are meant to become like that, like him.

But what means does the Spirit of God use to achieve that end? In what ways are we to co-operate with the Holy Spirit in his work of making us like Christ? I now gather together and express in a few words what has been written throughout this book about the ways in which we may work in partnership with the Spirit. We do it in five main ways; by trusting (faith), attending (devotion), trying (discipline), loving (fellowship) and growing (progress).

1. Trusting

The Christian life begins and continues with faith. If we are to bear fruit, we must first come to Christ and then continue to live in him. Becoming and being a Christian is a matter of faith from start to finish. At the outset, faith is putting our trust in the Lord Jesus Christ who died and rose again for us, and entrusting our lives to his care and keeping. United to him by faith, we continue to live in him by faith, *i.e.* by receptivity. A tree grows and bears fruit by what it takes in from its environment. We are to keep on receiving Christ and the life and food he continues to give. Trusting and receiving, we bear the fruit of Christlike character and conduct. This faith is kept alive by the second activity, devotion.

2. Attending

Pay attention please! This challenge may often have been made to you at school. In the school of life, the Spirit educates us as we pay attention to Christ. For when the mind is directed to and concentrated upon Christ, then the Christian is fully exposed to the transforming influence of Christ. So we must, in the words of a collect, 'ever have the pattern of his holy life before our eyes'. That's the purpose of the devotional life in its various forms. Through meditation and recollection, through private prayer and public worship, through the preaching of the Word and the celebration of the sacraments, we turn our eyes upon Jesus. As we contemplate him, the Spirit changes us into his likeness.

3. Trying

The fruit of the Spirit is produced by the Spirit, and what is required of us in the first place is not that we do something, but that we allow something to be done in us. Our action becomes a response to the prior action of God. But we are required to make that response. As St Augustine put it, 'Without God we cannot: without us God will not.' So make a strenuous effort, based upon God's act of deliverance and liberation in Christ, and his activity within us by the Holy Spirit. The effort required of us is both negative and positive. We accept the discipline of restraint and of practice, of saying *no* to our temptations and *yes* to our obligations. We are to keep on putting off the vices of the old nature, and to keep on putting on the virtues of the new nature. By daily discipline, we grow daily. To change the metaphor, God has called us to walk in the Spirit; he doesn't offer us any easy ride to heaven. The road to hell is easy. The way that leads to life, the way of renunciation and discipline, is hard (Mt. 7:13-14).

4. Loving

Paul writes, not about the fruits, but about the fruit of the Spirit. The fruit is love, and love is called into being and grows in the context of personal relationships. It is known in the community of those who love and are loved. The vine which bears fruit is the people of God. Within the fellowship created by the Spirit and in which he lives, his fruit is produced. So share fully in the common life, in the family, in the small Christian group, in the church, local and universal. For Christlikeness is not for the hermit in the desert, but for those who meet constantly to share the apostles' teaching and the common life, to break bread and to pray (Acts 2:42). God has called us into the fellowship of his Son, so that we may worship, serve and witness together, loving one another as Christ has loved us. His character takes shape in us, as we relate to, get on with, care for and work with others.

5. Growing

In this hectic age we are tempted to buy advertised goods because, it is claimed, they save time and effort, *instant* coffee, for example. Sometimes converts have been won by the offer of an instant Christ: one who solves all our problems and delivers us from all our faults, immediately. There are indeed some blessings which Christ gives instantly when we turn to him (*e.g.* forgiveness); but he doesn't make us like himself instantaneously. Like the slow growth of the foetus in the womb, so Christ's nature is formed in us (Gal. 4:19). It is also by a slow and long-drawn-out process that fruit is produced; it grows, matures, ripens. We have to wait for it with patience. So don't be discouraged if you seem to make slow progress. The Christian life is 'A Pilgrim's *Progress*', provided Christian keeps the end in view. On 'the day of the Lord', at the advent of Christ, we shall be 'filled with the fruits of righteousness'. When we see him, we shall be like him (Phil. 1:10-11; 1 Jn. 3:2).

The Lord Jesus expects us to bear fruit. Polycarp, bishop of Smyrna, had been a Christian for eighty-six years when, rather than deny Christ, he accepted martyrdom and gave up his 'body to be burned'. As a young man, he was a companion of John, the apostle John, who in the Upper Room had listened to Jesus speaking about those branches which, abiding in the vine, bear much fruit. In Greek *much fruit is polycarpos*. Perhaps Polycarp was given that new name at his baptism, in the hope that he would bear much fruit. That hope was fulfilled in the outcome of his life. Your name is not Polycarp; but the name could describe your character and the outcome of your life. Jesus Christ, the same today as yesterday, commands you, 'Go and bear fruit.'